CLOUD MIGRATION MASTERY

COMPLETE GUIDE TO SEAMLESS CLOUD INTEGRATION WITH AWS, MICROSOFT AZURE, VMWARE & NAVISITE

4 BOOKS IN 1

BOOK 1
CLOUD MIGRATION ESSENTIALS: A BEGINNER'S GUIDE TO AWS

BOOK 2
MASTERING MICROSOFT AZURE: ADVANCED STRATEGIES FOR CLOUD MIGRATION

BOOK 3
VMWARE VIRTUALIZATION: OPTIMIZING CLOUD MIGRATION FOR ENTERPRISES

BOOK 4
NAVIGATING NAVISITE: EXPERT TACTICS FOR SEAMLESS CLOUD INTEGRATION

ROB BOTWRIGHT

1

Published by Rob Botwright
Library of Congress Cataloging-in-Publication Data
ISBN 978-1-83938-773-9
Cover design by Rizzo

Disclaimer

The contents of this book are based on extensive research and the best available historical sources. However, the author and publisher make no claims, promises, or guarantees about the accuracy, completeness, or adequacy of the information contained herein. The information in this book is provided on an "as is" basis, and the author and publisher disclaim any and all liability for any errors, omissions, or inaccuracies in the information or for any actions taken in reliance on such information. The opinions and views expressed in this book are those of the author and do not necessarily reflect the official policy or position of any organization or individual mentioned in this book. Any reference to specific people, places, or events is intended only to provide historical context and is not intended to defame or malign any group, individual, or entity. The information in this book is intended for educational and entertainment purposes only. It is not intended to be a substitute for professional advice or judgment. Readers are encouraged to conduct their own research and to seek professional advice where appropriate. Every effort has been made to obtain necessary permissions and acknowledgments for all images and other copyrighted material used in this book. Any errors or omissions in this regard are unintentional, and the author and publisher will correct them in future editions.

BOOK 1 - CLOUD MIGRATION ESSENTIALS: A BEGINNER'S GUIDE TO AWS

BOOK 2 - MASTERING MICROSOFT AZURE: ADVANCED STRATEGIES FOR CLOUD MIGRATION

BOOK 3 - VMWARE VIRTUALIZATION: OPTIMIZING CLOUD MIGRATION FOR ENTERPRISES

BOOK 4 - NAVIGATING NAVISITE: EXPERT TACTICS FOR SEAMLESS CLOUD INTEGRATION

Welcome to "Cloud Migration Mastery," a comprehensive book bundle that serves as your complete guide to achieving seamless cloud integration with leading platforms such as AWS, Microsoft Azure, VMware, and NaviSite. In today's rapidly evolving digital landscape, businesses are increasingly turning to the cloud to drive innovation, enhance agility, and optimize performance. However, navigating the complexities of cloud migration requires a deep understanding of each platform's unique features, best practices, and advanced strategies. That's where this book bundle comes in.

Book 1, "Cloud Migration Essentials: A Beginner's Guide to AWS," lays the foundation for your cloud journey with a beginner-friendly introduction to Amazon Web Services. Whether you're new to the cloud or looking to refresh your knowledge, this book provides a clear roadmap for understanding key concepts, navigating AWS services, and executing successful cloud migration projects.

Book 2, "Mastering Microsoft Azure: Advanced Strategies for Cloud Migration," takes you to the next level with advanced strategies and insights tailored specifically for the Microsoft Azure platform. From identity management to AI and machine learning services, this book equips you with the knowledge and expertise needed to maximize the benefits of Azure for your organization.

Book 3, "VMware Virtualization: Optimizing Cloud Migration for Enterprises," explores the role of VMware virtualization technology in optimizing cloud migration for enterprise environments. With a focus on vSphere architecture, performance monitoring, and best practices, this book provides invaluable guidance for enterprises seeking to leverage VMware for their cloud migration initiatives.

Book 4, "Navigating NaviSite: Expert Tactics for Seamless Cloud Integration," completes the bundle by offering expert tactics and strategies for integrating seamlessly with NaviSite's cloud services. From industry solutions to security frameworks, this book empowers you to navigate the complexities of NaviSite and unlock its full potential for your organization's cloud integration efforts.

Whether you're a beginner looking to get started or an experienced professional seeking advanced strategies, "Cloud Migration Mastery" has *something for everyone. With practical insights, real-world examples, and expert guidance, this book bundle is your ultimate companion on the journey to achieving seamless cloud integration across multiple platforms.*

BOOK 1
CLOUD MIGRATION ESSENTIALS
A BEGINNER'S GUIDE TO AWS

ROB BOTWRIGHT

Cloud deployment models offer various options for organizations to deploy and manage their applications and services in the cloud. The three primary cloud deployment models are public cloud, private cloud, and hybrid cloud. Public cloud is a model where cloud services are provided over the internet by third-party providers. In a public cloud model, organizations can access computing resources, such as virtual machines, storage, and networking, on a pay-as-you-go basis, without the need to invest in and maintain physical infrastructure. Popular public cloud providers include AWS, Microsoft Azure, and Google Cloud Platform. Organizations can deploy their applications and services on public cloud platforms using CLI commands or through web-based interfaces provided by the cloud provider. Private cloud is a cloud deployment model where computing resources are dedicated to a single organization and are not shared with other organizations. In a private cloud model, organizations can deploy their applications and services on infrastructure located either on-premises or in a data center owned and operated by a third-party provider. Private clouds offer greater control and customization compared to public clouds but require more upfront investment in infrastructure and management. Organizations can deploy a private cloud using virtualization technologies such as VMware or OpenStack, along with management tools like VMware vSphere or OpenStack Horizon. Hybrid cloud is a cloud deployment model that combines elements of public and private clouds. In a hybrid cloud model, organizations can deploy some applications and services on a public cloud while keeping others on a private cloud or on-premises infrastructure. Hybrid clouds offer flexibility and scalability, allowing organizations to leverage the benefits of both public and private clouds based on their specific requirements. To deploy a hybrid cloud, organizations can use technologies such as cloud bursting, which allows them to dynamically scale their resources between public and private clouds based on demand. Additionally, organizations can use cloud management platforms to orchestrate workloads across multiple cloud environments seamlessly. Overall, cloud deployment models play a crucial role in helping organizations leverage the scalability, flexibility, and cost-effectiveness of cloud computing while meeting their specific business needs and requirements. By understanding the different cloud deployment models and how they can be deployed and managed, organizations can make informed decisions about their cloud strategy and optimize their use of cloud resources for maximum efficiency and   innovation. Cloud service models define the types of services offered by cloud providers and how they are delivered to users. The three primary cloud service models are Infrastructure as a Service (IaaS), Platform as a Service (PaaS), and Software as a Service (SaaS). IaaS is a cloud service model where cloud providers offer virtualized computing resources over the internet. In an IaaS model, organizations can rent virtual machines, storage, and networking infrastructure on a pay-as-you-go basis, eliminating the need to invest in and maintain physical hardware. Popular IaaS providers include AWS EC2, Microsoft Azure Virtual Machines, and Google Compute Engine. To deploy resources in an IaaS environment, users can use CLI commands such as "aws ec2 run-instances" to launch virtual machines or "az vm create" to create virtual machines in Azure. PaaS is a cloud service model where cloud providers offer a platform that allows developers to build, deploy, and manage applications without worrying about the underlying infrastructure. In a PaaS model, developers can focus on writing code and developing applications, while the cloud provider handles tasks such as provisioning servers, managing databases, and scaling resources automatically. Popular PaaS offerings include AWS Elastic Beanstalk, Microsoft

Azure App Service, and Google App Engine. To deploy applications in a PaaS environment, developers can use CLI commands such as "eb create" to create an Elastic Beanstalk application or "az webapp create" to create an Azure App Service application. SaaS is a cloud service model where cloud providers offer software applications over the internet on a subscription basis. In a SaaS model, users can access and use software applications hosted in the cloud without the need to install or maintain them locally. Popular SaaS applications include Salesforce, Office 365, and Google Workspace. To use SaaS applications, users can access them through web browsers or dedicated client applications provided by the cloud provider. Cloud service models offer different levels of abstraction and flexibility, allowing organizations to choose the right model based on their specific needs and requirements. While IaaS provides maximum control and customization, PaaS offers greater convenience and productivity for developers, and SaaS provides ready-to-use applications with minimal management overhead. By understanding the characteristics and capabilities of different cloud service models, organizations can effectively leverage cloud computing to innovate, scale, and drive business growth. Additionally, cloud service models continue to evolve, with providers introducing new features and capabilities to meet the changing needs of users and industries. As organizations increasingly adopt cloud computing, understanding the different cloud service models and how to deploy and manage them effectively becomes essential for success in today's digital economy.

Compute services play a crucial role in cloud computing, providing the foundation for running applications and workloads in the cloud. The compute services offered by cloud providers enable users to provision, manage, and scale virtualized computing resources on-demand. These resources include virtual machines, containers, and serverless computing platforms. Virtual machines (VMs) are one of the fundamental compute services provided by cloud providers. VMs allow users to create and run virtualized instances of servers in the cloud, providing the flexibility to deploy various operating systems and software applications. Cloud providers offer VMs in different configurations, including predefined instance types with varying amounts of CPU, memory, and storage resources. Users can deploy VMs using CLI commands such as "aws ec2 run-instances" in AWS or "az vm create" in Azure. Containers are another popular compute service that enables users to package and deploy applications along with their dependencies in lightweight, portable containers. Containers provide a more efficient and scalable alternative to traditional VMs, allowing for faster application deployment and resource utilization. Cloud providers offer container orchestration platforms such as Amazon ECS, Azure Kubernetes Service (AKS), and Google Kubernetes Engine (GKE) to manage containerized applications at scale. Users can deploy containerized applications using CLI commands such as "docker run" to run containers locally or "kubectl apply" to deploy Kubernetes resources. Serverless computing platforms, also known as Function as a Service (FaaS), allow users to run code in response to events without managing underlying server infrastructure. Serverless platforms automatically scale resources based on demand, enabling users to focus on writing code without worrying about provisioning or managing servers. Cloud providers offer serverless platforms such as AWS Lambda, Azure Functions, and Google Cloud Functions. Users can deploy serverless functions using CLI commands such as "aws lambda create-function" or "az functionapp create" to create and deploy functions in AWS Lambda or Azure Functions, respectively. In addition to these primary compute services, cloud providers offer a range of other compute services and features to meet the diverse needs of users and applications. These include GPU instances for accelerating graphics and compute-intensive workloads, FPGA instances for hardware acceleration, and custom machine types for optimizing performance and cost. Cloud providers also offer managed services for specific use cases, such as databases, analytics, and machine learning, which include built-in compute capabilities tailored to those services. Overall, compute services form the backbone of cloud computing, enabling organizations to build, deploy, and scale applications and workloads with ease and efficiency. By understanding the different compute services offered by cloud providers and how to deploy and manage them effectively, organizations can harness the full potential of cloud computing to drive innovation and business growth.

Storage and database services are foundational components of cloud computing, providing organizations with scalable and reliable solutions for storing and managing data. These services offer various storage options, including object storage, block storage, and file storage, as well as managed database services for different use cases and workloads. Object storage is a type of storage service that allows organizations to store and retrieve large amounts of unstructured data, such as images, videos, and documents, in a highly

scalable and durable manner. Object storage services, such as Amazon S3, Azure Blob Storage, and Google Cloud Storage, provide a simple and cost-effective solution for storing and serving static assets and media files in the cloud. Users can upload and manage objects in object storage using CLI commands such as "aws s3 cp" to copy files to and from Amazon S3 or "az storage blob upload" to upload blobs to Azure Blob Storage. Block storage, also known as persistent disk storage, provides organizations with high-performance storage volumes that can be attached to virtual machines to store operating system files, application data, and databases. Block storage services, such as Amazon EBS, Azure Disk Storage, and Google Cloud Persistent Disk, offer features such as snapshotting, encryption, and replication to ensure data integrity and availability. Users can create and manage block storage volumes using CLI commands such as "aws ec2 create-volume" to create volumes in Amazon EBS or "az disk create" to create disks in Azure Disk Storage. File storage is a type of storage service that allows organizations to store and share files and folders in a centralized and scalable manner. File storage services, such as Amazon EFS, Azure Files, and Google Cloud Filestore, provide network-attached storage (NAS) *solutions that can be accessed from multiple virtual machines or instances concurrently. Users can create and manage file shares using CLI commands such as "aws efs create-file-system" to create file systems in Amazon EFS or "az storage share create" to create file shares in Azure Files. Managed database services offer organizations fully managed and scalable database solutions that eliminate the need for database administration tasks such as provisioning, patching, and backups. These services provide built-in high availability, automatic scaling, and security features, allowing organizations to focus on building applications rather than managing databases. Managed database services include Amazon RDS, Azure SQL Database, and Google Cloud SQL for relational databases, as well as Amazon DynamoDB, Azure Cosmos DB, and Google Cloud Firestore for NoSQL databases. Users can create and manage managed databases using CLI commands such as "aws rds create-db-instance" to create database instances in Amazon RDS or "az sql db create" to create SQL databases in Azure SQL Database. In addition to these primary storage and database services, cloud providers offer a range of other storage and data management solutions to meet the diverse needs of organizations and applications. These include data warehousing services, content delivery networks (CDNs), and backup and archival solutions, which provide organizations with comprehensive tools and capabilities for storing, managing, and analyzing data in the cloud. By leveraging storage and database services effectively, organizations can build scalable, reliable, and cost-effective solutions that drive innovation and business growth in the digital age.*

Creating an AWS account is the first step towards accessing and using Amazon Web Services (AWS) cloud platform, enabling individuals and organizations to leverage a wide range of cloud services and resources for various use cases and workloads. The process of creating an AWS account is straightforward and can be completed in a few simple steps. To begin, you need to visit the AWS website and click on the "Create an AWS Account" button. This will take you to the AWS sign-up page, where you'll be prompted to provide your email address, password, and account name. Once you've entered this information, you'll need to verify your email address by clicking on the verification link sent to your inbox. After verifying your email address, you'll be asked to provide some additional information, such as your contact details, payment method, and identity verification. AWS requires a valid credit card or debit card to create an account, although some services offer a free tier with limited usage for new users. Once you've provided all the required information and completed the identity verification process, you can proceed to create your AWS account. During the account creation process, you'll be asked to choose a support plan, which determines the level of technical support and access to AWS resources available to you. AWS offers three support plans: Basic, Developer, and Business, with varying levels of support and pricing. After selecting a support plan, you'll need to review and accept the AWS Customer Agreement and the AWS Service Terms before finalizing your account creation. Once your account is created, you'll have access to the AWS Management Console, where you can manage your account settings, access billing and usage reports, and provision and manage AWS services and resources. The AWS Management Console provides a web-based interface for accessing and managing AWS services, but you can also use the AWS Command Line Interface (CLI) to interact with AWS programmatically. To install and configure the AWS CLI, you'll need to download and install the AWS CLI package for your operating system and configure it with your AWS credentials. Once the AWS CLI is installed and configured, you can use commands such as "aws configure" to set up your AWS credentials and "aws ec2 describe-instances" to list all EC2 instances in your account. In addition to the AWS CLI, you can also use the AWS Software Development Kits (SDKs) to integrate AWS services into your applications and automate common tasks. AWS offers SDKs for various programming languages, including Java, Python, JavaScript, and Ruby, which provide a convenient way to interact *with AWS services programmatically. Overall, creating an AWS account is the first step towards unlocking the full potential of AWS cloud platform, enabling you to build, deploy, and manage applications and workloads with ease and efficiency. By following the simple steps outlined above, you can quickly create an AWS account and start exploring the vast array of cloud services and resources available to you. Managing account settings in AWS is essential for ensuring security, compliance, and efficient resource utilization within your AWS environment. Account settings encompass a wide range of configurations and options that govern various aspects of your AWS account, including access management, billing preferences, and service limits. One of the primary account settings you'll encounter is Identity and Access Management (IAM), which allows you to manage user access to AWS services and resources. Using IAM, you can create and manage IAM users, groups, and roles, define fine-grained permissions using IAM policies, and enable multi-factor authentication (MFA) for added security. To manage IAM settings, you can use the AWS Management Console or the AWS CLI. For example, you can use the "aws iam create-user" command to create a new IAM user or "aws iam update-user" to update an existing IAM user's properties. Another important aspect of managing account settings is configuring* billing preferences and cost management options. AWS provides various tools and features for monitoring and controlling your AWS spending, such as AWS Budgets, AWS Cost Explorer, and AWS Cost and Usage Reports. By configuring billing alarms, setting up budget thresholds, and analyzing usage patterns, you can optimize your AWS spending and avoid unexpected charges. To manage billing preferences, you can use the AWS Billing and Cost Management Console or the AWS CLI. For instance, you can use the "aws ce get-cost-and-usage" command to retrieve cost and usage data for your account or "aws ce create-cost-alarm" to create a billing alarm based on predefined thresholds. Additionally, managing account settings involves configuring service limits and quotas to ensure that your AWS resources are appropriately sized and scaled to meet your needs. AWS imposes default service limits on resources such as EC2 instances, S3 buckets, and RDS database instances to prevent abuse and ensure fair resource allocation. You can view and request service limit increases using the AWS Service Quotas Console or the AWS Support Center. For example, you can use the "aws service-quotas get-service-quota" command to retrieve information about service quotas or "aws service-quotas request-service-quota-increase" to request a quota increase for a specific service. Security is paramount when managing account settings in

AWS, and implementing best practices for securing your account is essential to protect your data and resources from unauthorized access and breaches. This includes enabling AWS CloudTrail for auditing and logging API activity, configuring AWS Config for tracking resource configurations and changes, and implementing AWS Organizations for centralized management of multiple AWS accounts. You can use the AWS Management Console or the AWS CLI to configure these security features. For instance, you can use the "aws cloudtrail create-trail" command to create a new CloudTrail trail or "aws configservice put-configuration-recorder" to enable AWS Config recording. In addition to security measures, managing account settings also involves configuring networking and connectivity options to establish secure and reliable communication between your AWS resources and external networks. This includes configuring Virtual Private Cloud (VPC) settings, setting up network access control lists (ACLs) and security groups, and configuring VPN or Direct Connect connections for hybrid cloud deployments. You can use the AWS Management Console or the AWS CLI to manage networking settings. For example, you can use the "aws ec2 create-vpc" command to create a new VPC or "aws ec2 authorize-security-group-ingress" to configure inbound rules for a security group. Overall, managing account settings in AWS is a critical *aspect of cloud governance and administration, requiring careful consideration and attention to detail to ensure optimal performance, security, and cost-effectiveness of your AWS environment. By leveraging the tools and features provided by AWS and following best practices for account management, you can effectively manage your AWS account settings and maximize the value of your cloud investment.*

The AWS Management Console serves as the primary interface for interacting with and managing your AWS resources and services in the cloud. It provides a web-based graphical user interface (GUI) that allows users to access, configure, and monitor a wide range of AWS services and resources from a centralized dashboard. The AWS Management Console offers a user-friendly and intuitive experience, making it easy for both beginners and experienced users to navigate and manage their AWS environments efficiently. Upon logging into the AWS Management Console, users are presented with a dashboard that provides an overview of their account status, including billing and usage information, service health notifications, and recent activity. From the dashboard, users can access various services and resources organized into categories such as Compute, Storage, Database, Networking, Security, and Management Tools. Each service category contains a list of AWS services that users can explore and manage based on their specific needs and requirements. For example, the Compute category includes services such as Amazon EC2 (Elastic Compute Cloud) for virtual server hosting, Amazon ECS (Elastic Container Service) for container orchestration, and AWS Lambda for serverless computing. To access a specific service, users can simply click on its name or icon in the console dashboard, which will take them to the service's management console or landing page. Once inside a service's management console, users can perform various tasks such as creating, configuring, and managing resources, viewing usage and performance metrics, and accessing documentation and support resources. The AWS Management Console provides a consistent and unified experience across all AWS services, with common navigation elements and features that make it easy to switch between services and perform tasks seamlessly. For example, the top navigation bar includes links to commonly used services, as well as search functionality to quickly find specific services or resources. Additionally, the console sidebar provides access to various management tools and settings, such as IAM (Identity and Access Management), CloudFormation for infrastructure as code, and CloudWatch for monitoring and logging. In addition to the web-based interface, users can also interact with AWS services and resources programmatically using the AWS Command Line Interface (CLI) or AWS Software Development Kits (SDKs) for various programming languages. The AWS CLI provides a set of commands

that allow users to perform common tasks such as provisioning resources, querying service APIs, and managing configurations from the command line. For example, users can use the "aws ec2 create-instance" command to launch a new EC2 instance or "aws s3 ls" to list objects in an S3 bucket. Similarly, the AWS SDKs enable developers to integrate AWS services into their applications and automate workflows using programming languages such as Python, Java, JavaScript, and .NET. Overall, the AWS Management Console serves as a powerful and versatile tool for managing AWS resources and services, providing users with the flexibility and control they need to build, deploy, and scale applications in the cloud. Whether you're a beginner exploring AWS for the first time or an experienced cloud architect managing complex infrastructures, the console offers a rich set of features and capabilities to meet your needs and drive innovation in the cloud.
Customizing your console experience in AWS allows you to tailor the AWS Management Console to suit your preferences and workflow, enabling you to work more efficiently and effectively in the cloud. The AWS Management Console offers various customization options that allow you to personalize the look and feel of the console, organize your resources and services, and streamline common tasks. One of the most basic customization options

is the ability to change the color theme of the console. By default, the console uses a light theme, but you can switch to a dark theme for improved readability and reduced eye strain, especially during extended usage sessions. To change the color theme of the console, you can navigate to the settings menu in the top-right corner of the console, select "Preferences," and then choose your preferred theme from the available options. Another useful customization option is the ability to rearrange and organize the console dashboard to display the services and resources you use most frequently. You can customize the dashboard by adding, removing, and rearranging tiles to create a personalized view that reflects your workflow and priorities. To customize the dashboard, simply click on the "Customize dashboard" button on the dashboard page, then drag and drop tiles to rearrange them or click on the "+" icon to add new tiles for your favorite services. Additionally, you can create multiple dashboards for different use cases or projects and switch between them as needed. Another way to customize your console experience is by creating shortcuts to frequently accessed services and resources. The AWS Management Console allows you to create custom shortcuts to specific services or resources and add them to your browser's bookmarks bar for quick access. To create a shortcut, simply navigate to the desired service or resource in the console, then click on the browser's bookmark icon and save the page as a bookmark. You can then rename the bookmark and drag it to your bookmarks bar for easy access. Additionally, you can use keyboard shortcuts to navigate the console more efficiently and perform common tasks quickly. The AWS Management Console provides a set of keyboard shortcuts that allow you to navigate between pages, open and close menus, and perform other actions without using the mouse. To view the list of available keyboard shortcuts, you can press the "?" key while in the console, which will display a pop-up window with a list of keyboard shortcuts and their corresponding actions. Furthermore, you can customize keyboard shortcuts to suit your preferences by modifying the key bindings in your browser's settings. Another useful customization option is the ability to configure default settings and preferences for various AWS services. Many AWS services allow you to customize default settings such as region, instance type, and security settings, which can save you time and effort when provisioning resources. To configure default settings for a specific service, you can navigate to the service's settings page in the console, then select "Defaults" or "Preferences" to configure your preferred settings. Additionally, you can use AWS CloudFormation to create custom templates for provisioning resources with predefined configurations and settings.

CloudFormation allows you to define infrastructure as code using a declarative template language, which you can use to automate the deployment of complex architectures and configurations. To create a CloudFormation template, you can use the AWS Management Console, AWS Command Line Interface (CLI), or AWS Software Development Kits (SDKs) to define the resources and configurations you want to deploy, then save the template as a JSON or YAML file. You can then use the CloudFormation console or CLI to deploy the template and provision resources based on the defined configurations. Overall, customizing your console experience in AWS allows you to optimize your workflow, increase productivity, and make the most of the powerful features and capabilities offered by the AWS cloud platform. By personalizing the console to suit your preferences and requirements, you can work more efficiently and effectively in the cloud, enabling you to focus on building and innovating with confidence.

Launching an EC2 instance in AWS is a fundamental task that allows you to provision virtual servers in the cloud, enabling you to run applications and workloads with flexibility and scalability. The Elastic Compute Cloud (EC2) service is a core component of AWS, providing resizable compute capacity in the form of virtual machines known as instances. To launch an EC2 instance, you can use the AWS Management Console, AWS Command Line Interface (CLI), or AWS Software Development Kits (SDKs) for various programming languages. Using the AWS Management Console, you can navigate to the EC2 dashboard, click on the "Launch Instance" button, and follow the step-by-step wizard to configure and launch your instance. The wizard guides you through the process of selecting an Amazon Machine Image (AMI), choosing an instance type, configuring instance details such as networking and storage, and setting up security groups and key pairs. Alternatively, you can use the AWS CLI to launch an EC2 instance from the command line. The "aws ec2 run-instances" command allows you to specify parameters such as the AMI ID, instance type, subnet ID, security group

IDs, and key pair name to launch an instance with the desired configurations. For example, you can use the following command to launch a new EC2 instance with a specific AMI, instance type, and security group:

bash

Copy code

aws ec2 run-instances --image-id ami-12345678 --instance-type t2.micro --subnet-id subnet-12345678 --security-group-ids sg-12345678 --key-name my-keypair

This command creates a new EC2 instance using the specified AMI, instance type, subnet, security group, and key pair. Additionally, you can use the AWS SDKs to programmatically launch EC2 instances from your applications using languages such as Python, Java, JavaScript, and .NET. The SDKs provide a set of APIs that allow you to interact with AWS services and resources, including EC2, and perform actions such as launching instances, stopping instances, and managing instance lifecycle. For example, you can use the AWS SDK for Python (Boto3) to launch an EC2 instance with the following code:

python

Copy code

import boto3 ec2 = boto3.client('ec2') response = ec2.run_instances(ImageId='ami-12345678', InstanceType='t2.micro', MinCount=1, MaxCount=1,

SubnetId='subnet-12345678', SecurityGroupIds=['sg-12345678'], KeyName='my-keypair')
print(response)

This code creates a new EC2 client using Boto3, then calls the "run_instances" method to launch a new instance with the specified parameters. Once you've launched an EC2 instance, you can access it using SSH (Secure Shell) or RDP (Remote Desktop Protocol) depending on the operating system and configuration of the instance. For Linux instances, you can use SSH to connect to the instance using the private key associated with the key pair used during instance launch. For Windows instances, you can use RDP to connect to the instance using the administrator password generated during instance launch. To connect to a Linux instance using SSH, you can use the following command:

bash

Copy code

ssh -i /path/to/private-key.pem ec2-user@instance-ip-address

Replace "/path/to/private-key.pem" with the path to your private key file and "instance-ip-address" with the public IP address or DNS name of your instance. For Windows instances, you can use a remote desktop client such as Remote Desktop Connection on Windows or Remmina on Linux to connect to the instance using the public IP address or DNS name of the instance. Once connected to the instance, you can configure and manage it like any other server, including installing software, configuring services, and deploying applications. Additionally, you can use AWS features such as Elastic Block Store (EBS) volumes, Elastic IP addresses, and instance metadata to customize and optimize your EC2 instances for your specific use case and workload requirements. By launching EC2 instances in AWS, you can quickly and easily provision virtual servers in the cloud, enabling you to run applications and workloads with flexibility, scalability, and reliability. Whether you're deploying a single instance for testing and development or provisioning a fleet of instances for production workloads, EC2 provides the compute capacity you need to build and innovate with confidence in the cloud.

Configuring instance settings in AWS is a crucial step in customizing your virtual servers to meet the specific requirements of your applications and workloads. When launching an EC2 instance, you have the opportunity to specify various configuration options that determine the instance's behavior, performance, and security. One of the key configuration options is selecting the Amazon Machine Image (AMI) for your instance. An AMI is a pre-configured template that contains the operating system, software packages, and configuration

settings required to launch an instance. You can choose from a wide range of public AMIs provided by AWS, or you can create your own custom AMI with the software and configurations you need. To specify the AMI for your instance, you can use the "aws ec2 run-instances" command and include the "--image-id" parameter followed by the ID of the desired AMI. For example, you can use the following command to launch an instance with a specific AMI:
bash

Copy code

aws ec2 run-instances --image-id ami-12345678 --instance-type t2.micro --subnet-id subnet-12345678 --security-group-ids sg-12345678 --key-name my-keypair

In this command, "ami-12345678" is the ID of the AMI you want to use for your instance. Another important configuration option is selecting the instance type, which determines the CPU, memory, storage, and networking capacity of the instance. AWS offers a wide range of instance types optimized for different use cases and workloads, from general-purpose instances for versatile applications to compute-optimized instances for CPU-intensive tasks and memory-optimized instances for memory-intensive workloads. To specify the instance type for your instance, you can use the "--instance-type" parameter in the "aws ec2 run-instances" command. For example, you can use the following command to launch an instance with a specific instance type:

bash

Copy code

```
aws ec2 run-instances --image-id ami-12345678 --instance-type t2.micro --subnet-id subnet-12345678 --security-group-ids sg-12345678 --key-name my-keypair
```

In this command, "t2.micro" is the instance type you want to use for your instance. Additionally, you can configure various instance details such as networking, storage, and security settings when launching an EC2 instance. For example, you can specify the subnet ID, security group IDs, and key pair name using the appropriate parameters in the "aws ec2 run-instances" command. The subnet ID specifies the VPC subnet in which to launch the instance, the security group IDs specify the security groups to associate with the instance, and the key pair name specifies the name of the key pair to use for SSH access to the instance. By configuring these instance settings, you can ensure that your instances are deployed in the appropriate network environment, have the necessary security controls in place, and can be accessed securely using SSH or RDP. Additionally, you can customize the storage settings for your instances by attaching Amazon Elastic Block Store (EBS) volumes to provide persistent block-level storage. EBS volumes can be

attached to instances as additional storage devices and can be used to store data, operating system files, and application files. To attach an EBS volume to an instance, you can use the "aws ec2 attach-volume" command and specify the volume ID and instance ID. For example, you can use the following command to attach a volume with a specific volume ID to an instance with a specific instance ID:
bash

Copy code

```
aws ec2 attach-volume --volume-id vol-12345678 --instance-id i-12345678 --device /dev/sdf
```

In this command, "vol-12345678" is the ID of the EBS volume you want to attach, "i-12345678" is the ID of the instance to which you want to attach the volume, and "/dev/sdf" is the device name to assign to the volume on the instance. Additionally, you can configure instance settings such as instance metadata and user data to customize the behavior and configuration of your instances. Instance metadata provides information about the instance such as instance ID, public IP address, private IP address, and availability zone, which can be accessed from within the instance using HTTP requests. Instance user data allows you to pass custom initialization scripts and configuration data to your instances when they are launched, which can be used to automate instance setup and configuration tasks. To configure instance metadata *and user data, you can use the AWS Management Console, AWS CLI, or AWS SDKs. For example, you can use the "aws ec2 describe-instances" command to retrieve instance metadata, or you can use the "aws ec2 run-instances" command and include the "--user-data" parameter followed by the base64-encoded user data string. In summary, configuring instance settings in AWS is an essential aspect of deploying and managing EC2 instances, allowing you to customize your virtual servers to meet the specific requirements of your applications and workloads. By specifying the appropriate AMI, instance type, networking, storage, and security settings, you can ensure that your instances are deployed correctly and perform optimally in the AWS cloud. Additionally, you can leverage instance metadata and user data to automate instance setup and configuration tasks, further enhancing the efficiency and scalability of your AWS infrastructure.*

Amazon Simple Storage Service (S3) is a highly scalable and durable object storage service offered by Amazon Web Services (AWS), designed to store and retrieve any amount of data from anywhere on the web. It provides a simple and secure way to store data in the cloud, allowing you to offload storage infrastructure management and reduce operational overhead. S3 is built on a distributed architecture that automatically replicates data across multiple geographically dispersed data centers, ensuring high availability and durability of stored objects. One of the key features of Amazon S3 is its scalability, which allows you to store virtually unlimited amounts of data with virtually unlimited concurrent access. This makes S3 ideal for a wide range of use cases, including web hosting, data backup and archival, content distribution, and big data analytics. To get started with Amazon S3, you first need to create an S3 bucket, which serves as a container for storing objects. You can create an S3 bucket using the AWS Management Console, AWS CLI, or AWS SDKs. Using the AWS Management Console, you can navigate to the S3 dashboard, click on the "Create bucket" button, and follow the step-by-step wizard to configure your bucket settings.

Alternatively, you can use the "aws s3 mb" command in the AWS CLI to create a bucket from the command line. For example, you can use the following command to create a bucket with a specific name in a specific region:

bash

Copy code

aws s3 mb s3://my-bucket-name --region us-east-1

In this command, "my-bucket-name" is the name of the bucket you want to create, and "us-east-1" is the AWS region where you want to create the bucket. Once you've created an S3 bucket, you can start uploading objects to it. Objects in S3 are stored as key-value pairs, where the key is a unique identifier for the object and the value is the data itself. You can upload objects to an S3 bucket using the AWS Management Console, AWS CLI, or AWS SDKs. Using the AWS Management Console, you can navigate to the bucket you want to upload objects to, click on the "Upload" button, and follow the prompts to select and upload your files. Alternatively, you can use the "aws s3 cp" command in the AWS CLI to upload files to a bucket from the command line. For example, you can use the following command to upload a file to a bucket:

bash

Copy code

aws s3 cp /path/to/file.txt s3://my-bucket-name/file.txt

In this command, "/path/to/file.txt" is the path to the file you want to upload, and "s3://my-bucket-name/file.txt" is the S3 URI where you want to upload the file. Additionally, you can use S3's versioning feature to keep multiple versions of an object in the same bucket. Versioning helps protect against accidental deletion or modification of objects by maintaining a historical record of changes over time. You can enable versioning for an S3 bucket using the AWS Management Console or AWS CLI. Using the AWS Management Console, you can navigate to the bucket properties, click on the "Versioning" tab, and enable versioning for the bucket. Alternatively, you can use the "aws s3api put-bucket-versioning" command in the AWS CLI to enable versioning for a bucket. For example, you can use the following command to enable versioning for a bucket:

bash

Copy code

```
aws s3api put-bucket-versioning --bucket my-bucket-name --versioning-configuration Status=Enabled
```

In this command, "my-bucket-name" is the name of the bucket for which you want to enable versioning. Once versioning is enabled, S3 will automatically create a new version of an object whenever it is modified or deleted, allowing you to restore previous versions if needed. Additionally, you can use S3's lifecycle management feature to automatically archive or delete objects based on predefined rules. Lifecycle management helps reduce storage costs and streamline data management by automatically transitioning objects to lower-cost storage classes or deleting objects that are no longer needed. You can configure lifecycle rules for an S3 bucket using the AWS Management Console, AWS CLI, or AWS SDKs. Using the AWS Management Console, you can navigate to the bucket properties, click on the "Lifecycle" tab, and define lifecycle rules for the bucket. Alternatively, you can use the "aws s3api put-bucket-lifecycle" command in the AWS CLI to configure lifecycle rules for a bucket. For example, you can use the following command to configure a lifecycle rule that transitions objects to the Glacier storage class after 30 days:

bash

Copy code

```
aws s3api put-bucket-lifecycle --bucket my-bucket-name --lifecycle-configuration '{ "Rules": [ { "ID": "GlacierRule", "Prefix": "", "Status": "Enabled", "Transitions": [ { "Days": 30, "StorageClass": "GLACIER" } ] } ] }'
```

In this command, "my-bucket-name" is the name of the bucket for which you want to configure lifecycle rules, and "GLACIER" is the storage class to which objects will be transitioned after 30 days. Overall,

Amazon S3 is a powerful and versatile storage service that offers scalability, durability, and a wide range of features for storing and managing data in the cloud. By understanding the basics of S3 and how to configure and use its various features, you can leverage S3 to store and manage your data with confidence, ensuring high availability, durability, and cost-effectiveness for your applications and workloads.

Uploading and managing objects in Amazon S3 buckets is a fundamental aspect of utilizing the storage service for various data storage and management needs. Amazon S3 provides a straightforward and reliable method for uploading, organizing, and managing objects, which can include anything from individual files to large datasets and multimedia content. To begin uploading objects to an S3 bucket, you first need to have a bucket created within your AWS account. Buckets serve as containers for storing objects and can be created using the AWS Management Console, AWS CLI, or AWS SDKs. Using the AWS Management Console, you can navigate to the S3 dashboard, click on the "Create bucket" button, and follow the prompts to specify the bucket name and region. Alternatively, you can use the "aws s3 mb" command in the AWS CLI to create a bucket from the command line. For example, you can use the following command to create a bucket named "my-bucket" in the US East (Ohio) region:

bash

Copy code

aws s3 mb s3://my-bucket --region us-east-2

Once you have a bucket created, you can start uploading objects to it. Objects in S3 are stored as key-value pairs, where the key represents the unique identifier for the object within the bucket, and the value is the data itself. Uploading objects to an S3 bucket can be done using various methods, including the AWS Management Console, AWS CLI, or AWS SDKs. Using the AWS Management Console, you can navigate to the bucket you want to upload objects to, click on the "Upload" button, and follow the prompts to select and upload your files. Alternatively, you can use the "aws s3 cp" command in the AWS CLI to upload files to a bucket from the command line. For example, you can use the following command to upload a file named "example.txt" to the "my-bucket" bucket:

bash

Copy code

aws s3 cp example.txt s3://my-bucket/

In this command, "example.txt" is the name of the file you want to upload, and "s3://my-bucket/" is the S3 URI specifying the bucket and key (object name) where the file should be uploaded. Additionally, you can specify options such as encryption, storage class, and metadata when uploading objects to S3. For example, you can use the "--sse" parameter to enable server-side encryption (SSE) for uploaded objects, ensuring that data is encrypted at rest in S3. You can use various SSE options, including SSE-S3, SSE-KMS, and SSE-C, depending on your encryption requirements. Another option is to specify the storage class for uploaded objects using the "--storage-class" parameter. S3 offers different storage classes, such as STANDARD, STANDARD_IA (Standard-Infrequent Access), and GLACIER, each optimized for different access patterns and cost considerations. By default, objects are uploaded to the STANDARD storage class, but you can specify a different storage class based on your needs. Additionally, you can specify metadata for uploaded objects using the "--metadata" parameter, allowing you to include custom key-value pairs that provide additional information about the object. Once you've uploaded objects to an S3 bucket, you can manage them using various operations such as copying, moving, deleting, and retrieving objects. Using the AWS Management Console, you can navigate to the bucket and perform these operations interactively by selecting the objects and choosing the desired action from the menu. Alternatively, you can use the AWS CLI or AWS SDKs to perform these operations programmatically. For example, you can use the "aws s3 cp" command to copy objects between buckets or from local storage to S3, the "aws s3 mv" command to move objects within the same bucket or between buckets, and the "aws s3 rm" command to delete objects from a bucket. Additionally, you can use the "aws s3 ls" command to list objects in a bucket and the "aws s3 sync" command to synchronize files between a local directory and an S3 bucket. By mastering these object management techniques, you can efficiently organize and manage your data in S3, ensuring that it is easily accessible, secure, and cost-effective. Whether you're storing application data, website assets, or backup files, Amazon S3 provides a reliable and scalable solution for all your object storage needs in the cloud.

Virtual Private Cloud (VPC) is a fundamental building block of AWS cloud infrastructure, providing a logically isolated section of the AWS cloud where you can launch AWS resources in a virtual network that closely resembles a traditional network that you might operate in your data center. VPC allows you to define your own virtual network topology, including IP address ranges, subnets, route tables, and network gateways, giving you complete control over your network environment and providing a high level of security and isolation for your resources. When creating a VPC, you specify a range of IPv4 addresses for the VPC in the form of a CIDR block (Classless Inter-Domain Routing), such as 10.0.0.0/16, which defines the range of IP addresses available for instances launched in the VPC. You can create a VPC using the AWS Management Console, AWS CLI, or AWS SDKs. Using the AWS Management Console, you can navigate to the VPC dashboard, click on the "Create VPC" button, and follow the step-by-step wizard to specify the VPC settings, including the CIDR block, VPC name, and any optional features such as DNS hostname support. Alternatively, you can use the "aws ec2 create-vpc" command in the AWS CLI to create a VPC from the command line. For example, you can use the following command to create a VPC with the CIDR block 10.0.0.0/16:

bash

Copy code

```
aws ec2 create-vpc --cidr-block 10.0.0.0/16
```

In this command, "--cidr-block" specifies the CIDR block for the VPC. Once you have created a VPC, you can create subnets within the VPC to logically partition the IP address space and isolate resources within different availability zones (AZs) for fault tolerance and high availability. Subnets are associated with a specific AZ and can span multiple AZs within the same region. You can create subnets using the AWS Management Console, AWS CLI, or AWS SDKs. Using the AWS Management Console, you can navigate to the VPC dashboard, click on the "Subnets" tab, and click on the "Create subnet" button to specify the subnet settings, including the VPC, CIDR block, and AZ. Alternatively, you can use the "aws ec2 create-subnet" command in the AWS CLI to create a subnet from the command line. For example, you can use the following command to create a subnet with the CIDR block 10.0.1.0/24 in the VPC with the ID "vpc-12345678" and the AZ "us-east-1a":

bash

Copy code

aws ec2 create-subnet --vpc-id vpc-12345678 --cidr-block 10.0.1.0/24 --availability-zone us-east-1a

In this command, "--vpc-id" specifies the ID of the VPC, "--cidr-block" specifies the CIDR block for the subnet, and "--availability-zone" specifies the AZ for the subnet. Once you have created subnets within your VPC, you can configure route tables to control the routing of traffic between subnets and to the internet. Each subnet in a VPC is associated with a route table, which contains a set of rules, called routes, that determine where network traffic is directed. By default, a new VPC is created with a main route table that contains a local route for each subnet in the VPC, allowing communication between instances in the same VPC. You can create custom route tables and associate them with specific subnets to implement more advanced routing configurations, such as routing traffic to internet gateways (IGWs) for outbound internet access or to virtual private gateways (VGWs) for VPN connections to on-premises networks. You can create route tables using the AWS Management Console, AWS CLI, or AWS SDKs. Using the AWS Management Console, you can navigate to the VPC dashboard, click on the "Route Tables" tab, and click on the "Create route table" button to specify the route table settings, including the VPC. Alternatively, you can use the "aws ec2 create-route-table" command in the AWS CLI to create a route table from the command line. For example, you can use the following command to create a route table in the VPC with the ID "vpc-12345678":

bash

Copy code

```
aws ec2 create-route-table --vpc-id vpc-12345678
```

In this command, "--vpc-id" specifies the ID of the VPC for which you want to create the route table. Once you have created route tables, you can associate them with subnets using the AWS Management Console, AWS CLI, or AWS SDKs. Associating a route table with a subnet determines which route table is used for routing traffic to and from instances in the subnet. By default, each subnet is associated with the main route table for the VPC, but you can associate custom route tables with specific subnets to implement different routing configurations. Using the AWS Management Console, you can navigate to the subnet details page, click on the "Route table" tab, and click on the "Edit route table association" button to associate a route table with the subnet. Alternatively, you can use the "aws ec2 associate-route-table" command in the AWS CLI to associate a route table with a subnet from the command line. For example, you can use the following command to associate the route table with the ID "rtb-12345678" with the subnet with the ID "subnet-12345678":

bash

Copy code

```
aws ec2 associate-route-table --subnet-id subnet-12345678 --route-table-id rtb-12345678
```

In this command, "--subnet-id" specifies the ID of the subnet, and "--route-table-id" specifies the ID of the route table you want to associate with the subnet. Overall, understanding the fundamentals of VPC is essential for building secure, scalable, and highly available AWS cloud architectures. By mastering VPC concepts such as CIDR blocks, subnets, route tables, and route propagation, you can design and implement network environments that meet your specific requirements and enable you to deploy and manage AWS resources with confidence.

Configuring Virtual Private Cloud (VPC) networking components is a crucial step in designing and deploying network architectures in the AWS cloud, enabling you to create a secure and scalable network environment for your AWS resources. One *of the fundamental networking components of a VPC is the Internet Gateway (IGW), which provides a connection between your VPC and the internet, allowing instances within the VPC to communicate with resources on the internet and vice versa. To create an Internet Gateway, you can use the AWS Management Console, AWS CLI, or AWS SDKs. Using the AWS Management Console, you can navigate to the VPC dashboard, click on the "Internet Gateways" tab, and click on the "Create internet gateway" button to create a new IGW and attach it to your VPC. Alternatively, you can use the "aws ec2 create-internet-gateway" command in the AWS CLI to create an Internet Gateway from the command line. For example, you can use the following command to create an Internet Gateway:*

bash

Copy code

aws ec2 create-internet-gateway

Once you have created an Internet Gateway, you need to attach it to your VPC to enable internet connectivity for instances within the VPC. You can attach an Internet Gateway to a VPC using the AWS Management Console or AWS CLI. Using the AWS Management Console, you can navigate to the Internet Gateways page, select the Internet Gateway you want to attach, and choose the

"Attach to VPC" action from the menu to specify the VPC to attach it to. Alternatively, you can use the "aws ec2 attach-internet-gateway" command in the AWS CLI to attach an Internet Gateway to a VPC. For example, you can use the following command to attach an Internet Gateway with the ID "igw-12345678" to a VPC with the ID "vpc-12345678":

bash

Copy code

aws ec2 attach-internet-gateway --internet-gateway-id igw-12345678 --vpc-id vpc-12345678

In this command, "--internet-gateway-id" specifies the ID of the Internet Gateway, and "--vpc-id" specifies the ID of the VPC to which you want to attach it. Another essential networking component of a VPC is the Route Table, which defines the routing rules for traffic within the VPC and between the VPC and the internet. Each subnet in a VPC is associated with a route table, which contains a set of rules that determine where network traffic is directed. By default, each VPC comes with a main route table, which contains a local route for each subnet in the VPC, allowing communication between instances in the same VPC. However, you can create custom route tables and associate them with specific subnets to implement more advanced routing configurations.

To create a custom route table, you can use the AWS Management Console, AWS CLI, or AWS SDKs. Using the AWS Management Console, you can navigate to the Route Tables page, click on the "Create route table" button, and specify the VPC to associate it with. Alternatively, you can use the "aws ec2 create-route-table" command in the AWS CLI to create a route table from the command line. For example, you can use the following command to create a route table in a VPC with the ID "vpc-12345678":

bash

Copy code

```bash
aws ec2 create-route-table --vpc-id vpc-12345678
```

Once you have created a route table, you can define the routing rules by adding routes to it. You can add routes to a route table using the AWS Management Console, AWS CLI, or AWS SDKs. Using the AWS Management Console, you can navigate to the Route Tables page, select the route table you want to modify, and click on the "Edit routes" button to add or edit routes. Alternatively, you can use the "aws ec2 create-route" command in the AWS CLI to add a route to a route table from the command line. For example, you can use the following command to add a route to a route table with the ID "rtb-12345678" that directs traffic destined for the internet (0.0.0.0/0) to an Internet Gateway with the ID "igw-12345678":

bash

Copy code

```
aws ec2 create-route --route-table-id rtb-12345678 --destination-cidr-block 0.0.0.0/0 --gateway-id igw-12345678
```

In this command, "--route-table-id" specifies the ID of the route table, "--destination-cidr-block" specifies the destination CIDR block for the route, and "--gateway-id" specifies the ID of the gateway to which traffic should be routed. Additionally, you can associate subnets with route tables to determine which routing rules are applied to traffic originating from instances in the subnet. Each subnet is associated with a single route table, but you can change the association to use a different route table if needed. To associate a subnet with a route table, you can use the AWS Management Console, AWS CLI, or AWS SDKs. Using the AWS Management Console, you can navigate to the Subnets page, select the subnet you want to modify, and click on the "Edit route table association" button to specify the route table to associate with the subnet. Alternatively, you can use the "aws ec2 associate-route-table" command in the AWS CLI to associate a route table with a subnet from the command line. For

example, you can use the following command to associate a route table with the ID "rtb-12345678" with a subnet with the ID "subnet-12345678":
bash
Copy code

```
aws ec2 associate-route-table --subnet-id subnet-12345678 --route-table-id rtb-12345678
```

In this command, "--subnet-id" specifies the ID of the subnet, and "--route-table-id" specifies the ID of the route table to associate with the subnet. Overall, configuring VPC networking components is an essential aspect of building and managing network environments in the AWS cloud. By understanding how to create and configure Internet Gateways, Route Tables, and subnet associations, you can design secure, scalable, and highly available network architectures that meet the needs of your applications and workloads.

Identity and Access Management (IAM) is a foundational service in Amazon Web Services (AWS) that enables you to manage access to AWS resources securely. IAM allows you to control who can access your AWS resources and what actions they can perform on those resources. One of the key concepts in IAM is the use of identities, which represent the entities that interact with your AWS account, such as users, groups, and roles. Users are individual IAM entities that represent a person or application that interacts with AWS resources. You can create IAM users for individuals or applications that need access to your AWS account, and each user has its own set of security credentials, including an access key ID and a secret access key, that are used to authenticate requests to AWS. To create an IAM user, you can use the AWS Management Console, AWS CLI, or AWS SDKs. Using the AWS Management Console, you can navigate to the IAM dashboard, click on the "Users" tab, and click on the "Add user" button to create a new IAM user. Alternatively, you can use the "aws iam create-user" command in the AWS CLI to create a user from the command line. For example, you can use the following command to create a user named "john.doe":

bash

Copy code

aws iam create-user --user-name john.doe

In this command, "--user-name" specifies the username of the new IAM user. Groups are collections of IAM users that are treated as a single unit for the purposes of permissions management. You can create IAM groups to simplify permissions management by assigning permissions to groups rather than individual users. By adding users to groups, you can grant them the same set of permissions without having to manage permissions individually for each user. To create an IAM group, you can use the AWS Management Console, AWS CLI, or AWS SDKs. Using the AWS Management Console, you can navigate to the IAM dashboard, click on the "Groups" tab, and click on the "Create group" button to create a new IAM group. Alternatively, you can use the "aws iam create-group" command in the AWS CLI to create a group from the command line. For example, you can use the following command to create a group named "developers":

bash

Copy code

aws iam create-group --group-name developers

In this command, "--group-name" specifies the name of the new IAM group. Roles are another type of IAM entity that enables you to delegate permissions to entities outside of your AWS account. Roles are typically used to grant permissions to AWS services, such as EC2 instances or Lambda functions, so that they can perform actions on your behalf. You can also use roles to grant temporary access to users or applications that are not part of your AWS account. To create an IAM role, you can use the AWS Management Console, AWS CLI, or AWS SDKs. Using the AWS Management Console, you can navigate to the IAM dashboard, click on the "Roles" tab, and click on the "Create role" button to create a new IAM role. Alternatively, you can use the "aws iam create-role" command in the AWS CLI to create a role from the command line. For example, you can use the following command to create a role named "ec2-role" for use by EC2 instances:
bash
Copy code

```
aws iam create-role --role-name ec2-role --assume-role-policy-document file://trust-policy.json
```

In this command, "--role-name" specifies the name of the new IAM role, and "--assume-role-policy-document" specifies the JSON file containing the trust policy that defines which entities are allowed to assume the role. Once you have created IAM users, groups, and roles, you can assign permissions to them using IAM policies. IAM policies are JSON documents that define permissions using a set of policy statements, each of which specifies a set of actions, resources, and conditions. You can attach policies to IAM users, groups, and roles to grant or deny permissions to perform actions on specific AWS resources. To create an IAM policy, you can use the AWS Management Console, AWS CLI, or AWS SDKs. Using the AWS Management Console, you can navigate to the IAM dashboard, click on the "Policies" tab, and click on the "Create policy" button to create a new IAM policy. Alternatively, you can use the "aws iam create-policy" command in the AWS CLI to create a policy from the command line. For example, you can use the following command to create a policy named "s3-read-only" that grants read-only access to objects in an S3 bucket:

bash

Copy code

```
aws iam create-policy --policy-name s3-read-only --policy-document file://s3-read-only-policy.json
```

In this command, "--policy-name" specifies the name of the new IAM policy, and "--policy-document" specifies the JSON file containing the policy document that defines the permissions. Once you have created an IAM policy, you can attach it to IAM users, groups, or roles to grant them the permissions defined in the policy. You can attach policies using the AWS Management Console, AWS CLI, or AWS SDKs. Using the AWS Management Console, you can navigate to the IAM dashboard, select the user, group, or role to which you want to attach the policy, click on the "Permissions" tab, and click on the "Add permissions" button to attach the policy. Alternatively, you can use the "aws iam attach-policy" command in the AWS CLI to attach a policy from the command line. For example, you can use the following command to attach the "s3-read-only" policy to the "john.doe" user:

bash

Copy code

```
aws iam attach-policy --policy-arn arn:aws:iam::123456789012:policy/s3-read-only --user-name john.doe
```

In this command, "--policy-arn" specifies the ARN (Amazon Resource Name) of the policy to attach, and "--user-name" specifies the username of the IAM user. Overall, understanding the basics of IAM is essential for managing access to your AWS resources securely and efficiently. By mastering IAM concepts such as users, groups, roles, and policies, you can effectively control who can access your AWS resources and what actions they can perform, ensuring the security and integrity of your cloud environment.

Implementing Security Groups and Network Access

Control Lists (ACLs) is essential for securing your Amazon Web Services (AWS) infrastructure and controlling inbound and outbound traffic to and from your instances. Security Groups act as virtual firewalls for your instances, controlling inbound and outbound traffic based on security rules that you define. Each security group acts as a set of firewall rules for one or more instances, allowing you to specify the type of traffic that is allowed to reach your instances. To create a security group, you can use the AWS Management Console, AWS CLI, or AWS SDKs. Using the AWS Management Console, you can navigate to the EC2 dashboard, click on the "Security Groups" tab, and click on the "Create security group" button to create a new security group. Alternatively, you can use the "aws ec2 create-security-group" command in the AWS CLI to create a security group from the command line. For example, you can use the following command to create a security group named "web-sg" with an inbound rule allowing HTTP traffic (port 80) from anywhere:

bash
Copy code

```
aws ec2 create-security-group --group-name web-sg --description "Security group for web servers"
```

In this command, "--group-name" specifies the name of the security group, and "--description" provides a description of the security group. Once you have created a security group, you can define inbound and outbound rules to control traffic to and from your instances. Inbound rules allow traffic to reach your instances, while outbound rules control the traffic that is allowed to leave your instances. You can add rules to a security group using the AWS Management Console, AWS CLI, or AWS SDKs. Using the AWS Management Console, you can navigate to the security group's details page, click on the "Inbound rules" or "Outbound rules" tab, and click on the "Edit rules" button to add or modify rules. Alternatively, you can use the "aws ec2 authorize-security-group-ingress" and "aws ec2 authorize-security-group-egress" commands in the AWS CLI to add rules from the command line. For example, you can use the following command to add an inbound rule allowing SSH traffic (port 22) from a specific IP address range (CIDR block) to the "web-sg" security group:

bash

Copy code

```bash
aws ec2 authorize-security-group-ingress --group-name web-sg --protocol tcp --port 22 --cidr 203.0.113.0/24
```

In this command, "--protocol" specifies the protocol for the rule (in this case, TCP), "--port" specifies the port range for the rule, and "--cidr" specifies the CIDR block for the allowed IP addresses. Network Access Control Lists (ACLs) are another layer of security that you can use to control traffic to and from subnets in your VPC. Network ACLs act as a firewall for controlling traffic at the subnet level, allowing you to define rules that govern inbound and outbound traffic based on IP addresses, protocols, and ports. To create a network ACL, you can use the AWS Management Console, AWS CLI, or AWS SDKs. Using the AWS Management Console, you can navigate to the VPC dashboard, click on the "Network ACLs" tab, and click on the "Create network ACL" button to create a new network ACL. Alternatively, you can use the "aws ec2 create-network-acl" command in the AWS CLI to create a network ACL from the command line. For example, you can use the following command to create a network ACL named "web-acl" in a VPC with the ID "vpc-12345678":

bash

Copy code

```
aws ec2 create-network-acl --vpc-id vpc-12345678 --tag-specifications 'ResourceType=network-acl,Tags=[{Key=Name,Value=web-acl}]'
```

In this command, "--vpc-id" specifies the ID of the VPC in which to create the network ACL, and "--tag-specifications" specifies tags to apply to the network ACL for easy identification. Once you have created a network ACL, you can define inbound and outbound rules to control traffic to and from the associated subnets. Inbound rules allow traffic to reach *instances in the subnet, while outbound rules control the traffic that is allowed to leave the subnet. You can add rules to a network ACL using the AWS Management Console, AWS CLI, or AWS SDKs. Using the AWS Management Console, you can navigate to the network ACL's details page, click on the "Inbound rules" or "Outbound rules" tab, and click on the "Edit rules" button to add or modify rules. Alternatively, you can use the "aws ec2 create-network-acl-entry" command in the AWS CLI to add rules from the command line. For example, you can use the following command to add an inbound rule allowing HTTP traffic (port 80) from any source to the "web-acl" network ACL:*

bash

Copy code

aws ec2 create-network-acl-entry --network-acl-id acl-12345678 --rule-number 100 --protocol tcp -- port-range From=80,To=80 --cidr-block 0.0.0.0/0 -- rule-action allow

In this command, "--network-acl-id" specifies the ID of the network ACL, "--rule-number" specifies the order in which the rule is evaluated (lower numbers are evaluated first), "--protocol" specifies the protocol for the rule (in this case, TCP), "--port-range" specifies the port range for the rule, "--cidr-block" specifies the CIDR block for the allowed IP addresses, and "--rule-action" specifies whether to allow or deny traffic that matches the rule. Overall, implementing Security Groups and Network ACLs is crucial for securing your AWS infrastructure and controlling traffic to and from your instances and subnets. By defining security rules that restrict access to only necessary ports and protocols, you can minimize the risk of unauthorized access and protect your resources from potential security threats.

Troubleshooting common AWS issues is an essential skill for effectively managing and maintaining your cloud infrastructure, as it allows you to quickly identify and resolve problems that may impact the performance, availability, or security of your resources and applications. One common issue that AWS users encounter is connectivity problems with EC2 instances, which can occur for various reasons, such as incorrect security group rules, network ACL settings, or routing table configurations. To troubleshoot connectivity issues with an EC2 instance, you can use the AWS Management Console or AWS CLI to check the security group rules and network ACL settings associated with the instance, ensuring that the necessary inbound and outbound traffic is allowed. Additionally, you can use the "aws ec2 describe-instances" command to retrieve information about the instance, including its network interfaces and associated security groups, to help diagnose the issue. Another common issue that AWS users face is performance degradation or latency in their applications, which can be caused by factors such as insufficient compute or storage resources, misconfigured services, or network bottlenecks. To troubleshoot performance issues in

AWS, you can use CloudWatch Metrics to monitor key performance indicators (KPIs) such as CPU utilization, memory usage, disk I/O, and network traffic for your resources and applications. You can also use CloudWatch Logs to analyze log data and identify any errors or exceptions that may be affecting performance. Additionally, you can use AWS Trusted Advisor to analyze your AWS environment and provide recommendations for optimizing performance, reducing costs, and improving security and reliability. Another common issue that AWS users encounter is resource exhaustion, which occurs when resources such as EC2 instances, RDS databases, or S3 buckets reach their limits or quotas, leading to service disruptions or downtime. To troubleshoot resource exhaustion issues in AWS, you can use the AWS Management Console or AWS CLI to check the current usage and limits for your resources, ensuring that you have sufficient capacity to meet your workload requirements. You can also use AWS CloudWatch Alarms to monitor resource usage and trigger notifications or automated actions when usage exceeds predefined thresholds. Additionally, you can use AWS Auto Scaling to automatically adjust the capacity of your resources based on demand, ensuring that you have enough capacity to handle fluctuations in workload without over-provisioning or under-provisioning resources. Another common issue that AWS users face is data loss or corruption, which can occur due to accidental deletion, hardware failure, software bugs, or security breaches. To troubleshoot data loss or corruption issues in AWS, you can use AWS Backup to create and manage backups of your data, ensuring that you have a reliable and scalable solution for protecting your critical data assets. You can also use AWS CloudTrail to log and monitor API activity in your AWS account, enabling you to track changes to your resources and identify any unauthorized or suspicious activity that may indicate a security breach. Additionally, you can use AWS Config to continuously assess the configuration of your AWS resources and detect any deviations from your desired configuration, helping you to identify and remediate security vulnerabilities or compliance issues before they impact your business. Another common issue that AWS users encounter is billing discrepancies or unexpected charges, which can occur due to factors such as unused resources, inefficient resource usage, or data transfer costs. To troubleshoot billing issues in AWS, you can use the AWS Management Console or AWS CLI to review your billing and usage reports, identifying any services or resources that are driving up costs or contributing to unexpected charges. You can also use AWS Budgets to set cost and usage budgets for your AWS account, enabling you to monitor spending and receive alerts when you exceed your budgeted amounts. Additionally, you can use AWS Cost Explorer to analyze your historical spending patterns and forecast future costs, helping you to optimize your AWS usage and reduce your overall cloud expenses. Overall, troubleshooting common AWS issues requires a combination of technical skills, operational expertise, and familiarity with AWS services and best practices. By leveraging the tools and techniques available in AWS, you can quickly diagnose and resolve issues, minimize downtime, and ensure the reliability and performance of your cloud infrastructure and applications.

Planning your cloud migration strategy is a critical step in the journey towards transitioning your IT infrastructure and applications to the cloud, as it lays the foundation for a successful migration by defining clear objectives, identifying potential risks and challenges, and outlining the steps and resources needed to execute the migration effectively. One of the first steps in planning your cloud migration strategy is to assess your existing IT environment and infrastructure to understand your current state and identify the workloads, applications, and data that are candidates for migration to the cloud. You can use tools such as AWS Application Discovery Service or third-party solutions like CloudScape to analyze your on-premises environment and collect data about your servers, storage, network, and applications, helping you to identify dependencies, usage patterns, and performance metrics that will inform your migration strategy. Once you have assessed your current environment, you can begin to define your cloud migration goals and objectives, which may include reducing infrastructure costs, improving scalability and flexibility, enhancing security and compliance, or accelerating innovation and time-to-market. By establishing clear goals and objectives for your cloud migration, you can align your migration strategy with your business priorities and ensure that the migration delivers tangible value and benefits to your organization. With your goals and objectives in mind, you can then begin to prioritize and categorize your workloads and applications based on factors such as business criticality, complexity, dependencies, and regulatory requirements. You can use tools such as AWS Migration Hub or the AWS Total Cost of Ownership (TCO) Calculator to assess the cost and complexity of migrating each workload and identify the most suitable migration approach for each workload, whether it be rehosting (lift and shift), re-platforming (lift, tinker, and shift), refactoring (re-architecting), repurchasing (replacing with SaaS), or retiring (decommissioning). Once you have prioritized your workloads and determined the most appropriate migration approach for each workload, you can begin to develop a detailed migration plan that outlines the specific tasks, timelines, dependencies, and resources needed to execute the migration successfully. Your migration plan should include a detailed project schedule that identifies key milestones, checkpoints, and deliverables, as well as a risk management plan that outlines potential risks and mitigation strategies for each phase of the migration. You can use project management tools such as Jira, Trello, or Microsoft Project to create and manage your migration plan, enabling you to track progress, communicate updates, and collaborate with stakeholders throughout the migration process. As you develop your migration plan, it is important to consider the people, processes, and technology aspects of your migration, as well as the impact on your organization's culture, skills, and operations. You can use change management frameworks such as ADKAR (Awareness, Desire, Knowledge, Ability, Reinforcement) or Kotter's 8-Step Process for Leading Change to manage the human side of the migration and ensure that your organization is prepared for the changes and challenges that come with migrating to the cloud. Additionally, you can leverage AWS Professional Services or engage with AWS Partners to access expertise, best practices, and resources to help you plan and execute your migration effectively. Once your migration plan is in place, you can begin to execute the migration in a phased approach, starting with low-risk, non-production workloads and gradually moving towards more complex, mission-critical workloads. You can use AWS services such as AWS Server Migration Service (SMS), AWS Database Migration Service (DMS), and AWS DataSync to migrate your servers, databases, and data to the cloud, ensuring minimal downtime, data loss, and disruption to your business operations. Throughout the migration process, it is important to monitor and measure the performance, availability, and cost of your migrated workloads and applications, and make adjustments as needed to optimize performance, minimize costs, and ensure compliance with your business requirements. You can use AWS CloudWatch, AWS CloudTrail, and AWS Config to monitor and audit your cloud infrastructure and applications, enabling you to identify and address any issues or deviations from your desired state in real-time. Additionally, you can use AWS Cost Explorer and AWS Budgets to track and analyze your cloud spending, enabling you to optimize costs and maximize the value of your cloud investment. As you complete the migration of your workloads and applications to the cloud, it is important to conduct a post-migration review to evaluate the success of the migration and identify any lessons learned or areas for improvement. You can use tools such as AWS Migration Hub or AWS Migration Evaluator (formerly TSO Logic) to assess the performance, cost, and compliance of your migrated workloads and applications, and validate that your migration goals and objectives have been achieved. By conducting a thorough post-migration review, you can capture valuable insights and feedback that will inform future migrations and enable you to continuously improve your cloud migration strategy and execution. Overall, planning your cloud migration strategy is a complex and iterative process that requires careful consideration of your business goals, technical requirements, and organizational capabilities. Executing a successful migration plan is a multifaceted process that requires meticulous planning, effective communication, and diligent execution to ensure a smooth transition from the current state to the desired state. One of the first steps in executing a successful migration plan is to communicate the plan to all stakeholders involved in the migration, including business leaders, IT teams, and end users, to ensure alignment and commitment to the migration goals and objectives. You can use communication tools such as email, meetings, and collaboration platforms like Slack or Microsoft Teams to disseminate information about the migration plan, including key milestones, timelines, and responsibilities. Additionally, you can use project management tools such as Asana or Jira to create and track tasks, assign responsibilities, and monitor progress throughout the migration process, enabling you to keep stakeholders informed and engaged. Once the migration plan has been communicated and agreed upon, you can begin to execute the plan by following the predefined tasks, timelines, and dependencies outlined in the plan. You can use the AWS Migration Hub or third-party *migration tools like CloudEndure or RiverMeadow to orchestrate and manage the migration of your workloads and applications to the cloud, ensuring that each migration task is completed efficiently and with minimal disruption to your business operations. As you execute the migration plan, it is important to closely monitor the progress of each migration task and address any issues or obstacles that arise in a timely manner to prevent delays or setbacks. You can use AWS CloudWatch and AWS Config to monitor the performance, availability, and compliance of your migrated workloads and applications in real-time, enabling you to identify and troubleshoot any issues before they impact your business operations. Additionally, you can use AWS CloudTrail to log and audit API activity in your AWS account, providing visibility into changes made to your cloud resources and helping you to maintain security and compliance throughout the migration process. As part of the migration execution process, it is important to conduct thorough testing of your migrated workloads and applications to ensure that they perform as expected and meet the required performance, availability, and security standards. You can use testing tools such as AWS CodeBuild, AWS CodeDeploy, and AWS CodePipeline to automate the testing and deployment of your applications in the cloud, enabling you to quickly identify and address any issues or defects before they impact your production environment. Additionally, you can use load testing tools like Apache JMeter or Gatling to simulate real-world traffic and measure the performance of your applications under different load conditions, helping you to identify and optimize performance bottlenecks before they affect end users. Throughout the migration execution process, it is important to communicate regularly with stakeholders and provide updates on the progress of the migration, including any challenges or issues that arise and the steps being taken to address them. You can use status reports, dashboards, and project updates to keep stakeholders informed and engaged, enabling them to provide feedback and support as needed to ensure the success of the migration. As you near the completion of the migration, it is important to conduct a final review to validate that all migration tasks have been completed successfully and that the migrated workloads and applications are functioning as expected in the cloud environment. You can use tools like AWS CloudFormation or AWS Systems Manager to automate the provisioning and configuration of your cloud resources, ensuring consistency and repeatability across your environment and reducing the risk of configuration errors or misconfigurations. Additionally, you can use AWS CloudTrail and AWS Config to audit and monitor changes to your cloud resources, providing visibility into who made the changes and when they were made, helping you to maintain security and compliance in your cloud environment. Once the migration is complete, you can begin to decommission any remaining on-premises infrastructure and finalize the transition to the cloud, ensuring that all necessary data, applications, and services have been migrated and that any dependencies or integrations have been updated or reconfigured to work in the cloud environment. By following a structured approach and leveraging the tools and resources available in AWS, you can execute a successful migration plan that delivers tangible benefits and value to your organization, including cost savings, scalability, and agility, while minimizing disruption to your business operations.*

BOOK 2
MASTERING MICROSOFT AZURE
ADVANCED STRATEGIES FOR CLOUD MIGRATION

ROB BOTWRIGHT

Microsoft Azure, often simply referred to as Azure, is a cloud computing platform and service offered by Microsoft that provides a wide range of cloud services, including computing, storage, networking, analytics, and more, enabling organizations to build, deploy, and manage applications and services in the cloud. Azure is one of the leading cloud providers in the industry, competing with other major players such as Amazon Web Services (AWS) and Google Cloud Platform (GCP), and it offers a comprehensive set of services and tools to meet the diverse needs of businesses and developers. One of the key features of Azure is its global network of data centers, which span across multiple regions and availability zones around the world, allowing customers to deploy their applications and services closer to their users for lower latency and improved performance. Azure offers a wide range of compute services, including virtual machines (VMs), containers, serverless computing, and more, enabling organizations to run a variety of workloads and applications in the cloud. Azure Virtual Machines (VMs) allow you to deploy and manage virtualized Windows and Linux servers in the cloud, providing flexibility and scalability to meet your computing needs. You can use the Azure portal or the Azure CLI (Command-Line Interface) to create and manage virtual machines in Azure, specifying parameters such as VM size, operating system, disk type, and networking configuration. Additionally, Azure offers a variety of container services, including Azure Kubernetes Service (AKS) and Azure Container Instances (ACI), which enable you to deploy and manage containerized applications in the cloud, providing agility and scalability for modern application development and deployment. Azure Functions is a serverless compute service that enables you to run event-driven code without managing infrastructure, allowing you to focus on building and deploying applications without worrying about underlying infrastructure management. With Azure Functions, you can execute code in response to events such as HTTP requests, queue messages, or timer triggers, enabling you to build scalable and cost-effective applications that automatically scale based on demand. In addition to compute services, Azure provides a variety of storage services, including Azure Blob Storage, Azure Files, Azure Disk Storage, and Azure Data Lake Storage, which enable you to store and manage data in the cloud at scale. Azure Blob Storage is a massively scalable object storage service that allows you to store and serve large amounts of unstructured data, such as images, videos, and documents, in the cloud. You can use the

Azure portal, Azure CLI, or Azure SDKs to create and manage Blob Storage accounts, upload and download data, and configure access controls and encryption settings for your data. Azure also offers a variety of networking services, including Virtual Network (VNet), Azure Load Balancer, Azure VPN Gateway, and Azure Application Gateway, which enable you to build secure and scalable network architectures in the cloud. Azure Virtual Network (VNet) is a foundational networking service that allows you to create isolated and secure network environments in Azure, enabling you to connect your Azure resources to each other and to your on-premises network securely. You can use the Azure portal or the Azure CLI to create and manage virtual networks in Azure, configure subnets, route tables, and network security groups, and establish connectivity to your on-premises network using VPN or ExpressRoute connections. Azure Load Balancer is a Layer 4 (TCP/UDP) load balancer that distributes incoming network traffic across multiple VMs or instances to ensure high availability and reliability of your applications and services. You can use the Azure portal or the Azure CLI to create and configure load balancers in Azure, specify backend pool targets, configure health probes, and define load balancing rules to distribute traffic based on various criteria such as round-robin or least connections. Azure also provides a variety of data services and analytics tools, including Azure SQL Database, Azure Cosmos DB, Azure Synapse Analytics, and Azure Machine Learning, which enable you to store, analyze, and derive insights from your data in the cloud. Azure SQL Database is a fully managed relational database service that allows you to build, scale, and manage relational databases in the cloud with ease. You can use the Azure portal, Azure CLI, or Azure PowerShell to create and manage SQL Database instances, configure performance and scalability options, and implement advanced security and compliance controls for your databases. Azure Cosmos DB is a globally distributed, multi-model database service that enables you to build highly responsive and scalable applications with low latency and high availability. You can use the Azure portal or the Azure CLI to create and manage Cosmos DB accounts, define data models and consistency levels, and configure geo-replication and partitioning strategies to optimize performance and reliability for your applications. Azure Synapse Analytics is an analytics service that enables you to analyze large volumes of data and derive insights from it using a combination of data warehousing and big data analytics capabilities. You can use the Azure portal or the Azure CLI to create and manage Synapse workspaces, ingest and transform data from various sources, and build and deploy machine learning models to uncover patterns and trends in your data. Azure Machine Learning is a cloud-based machine learning service that enables you to build, train, and deploy machine learning models at scale, using a variety of tools and frameworks such as TensorFlow, PyTorch, and scikit-learn. You can use the Azure portal, Azure CLI, or Azure SDKs to create and manage machine learning workspaces, develop and experiment with machine learning models using Jupyter notebooks or Azure Machine Learning Studio, and deploy models as web services or containerized applications for real-time inference. In addition to compute, storage, networking, and data services, Azure also provides a variety of management and monitoring tools, including Azure Monitor, Azure Security Center, Azure Policy, and Azure Resource Manager, which enable you to monitor, secure, and govern your Azure resources and applications effectively. Azure Monitor is a comprehensive monitoring service that allows you to collect, analyze, and visualize telemetry data from your Azure resources and applications, enabling you to identify and troubleshoot performance issues, optimize resource utilization, and ensure the reliability and availability of your applications. You can use the Azure portal, Azure CLI, or Azure REST APIs to configure monitoring settings, create custom metrics and alerts, and integrate with third-party monitoring tools such as

Grafana or Prometheus to extend monitoring capabilities further. Azure Security Center is a unified security management service that provides advanced threat protection, vulnerability management, and security posture assessment for your Azure resources and workloads. You can use the Azure portal or the Azure CLI to enable Security Center for your Azure subscriptions, configure security policies and recommendations, and remediate security vulnerabilities and misconfigurations to protect your cloud environment from cyber threats and attacks. Azure Marketplace and partnerships play a crucial role in expanding the ecosystem of services and solutions available on the Azure platform, offering customers a wide range of options to enhance their cloud experience and meet their specific business needs. Azure Marketplace serves as a one-stop shop for discovering, deploying, and managing a variety of third-party applications, solutions, and services, allowing customers to find and purchase software and services from trusted vendors and partners in the Azure ecosystem. With Azure Marketplace, customers can easily find and deploy pre-configured virtual machine images, container images, software appliances, and managed applications, enabling them to quickly spin up and provision resources for their workloads and applications without the need for manual configuration or setup. Customers can use the Azure portal, Azure CLI, or Azure PowerShell to browse the Azure Marketplace catalog, search for specific products and solutions, and deploy them directly to their Azure subscription with just a few clicks or commands. Additionally, Azure Marketplace offers a variety of deployment options, including pay-as-you-go, bring-your-own-license (BYOL), and free trials, allowing customers to choose the pricing and licensing model that best fits their budget and requirements. Azure Marketplace offers a wide range of categories and industries, including security, networking, analytics, artificial intelligence (AI), Internet of Things (IoT), and more, enabling customers to find and deploy solutions for virtually any use case or scenario. For example, customers can find and deploy security solutions such as firewall appliances, intrusion detection systems, and antivirus software to protect their Azure resources and applications from cyber threats and attacks. Similarly, customers can find and deploy analytics solutions such as data visualization tools, business Intelligence platforms, and machine learning models to gain insights and derive value from their data in the cloud. In addition to third-party solutions, Azure Marketplace also offers a variety of Azure services and offerings from Microsoft, including Azure Virtual Machines, Azure SQL Database, Azure Kubernetes Service (AKS), Azure Functions, and more, enabling customers to leverage the full power and capabilities of the Azure platform to build, deploy, and manage their applications and workloads in the cloud. Azure Marketplace is also home to a vibrant ecosystem of partners, including independent software vendors (ISVs), system integrators (SIs), managed service providers (MSPs), and consulting firms, who offer a wide range of services and expertise to help customers design, deploy, and optimize their Azure solutions. Partners can list their products and services on Azure Marketplace to reach a broader audience of Azure customers and drive adoption and usage of their offerings. Additionally, partners can leverage the Azure Partner Program and co-sell opportunities to collaborate with Microsoft sales teams and generate leads and revenue for their businesses. Microsoft works closely with its partners to enable them to build and deliver innovative solutions on the Azure platform, providing resources, tools, training, and support to help partners accelerate their growth and success in the cloud market. Partners can access technical resources and documentation through the Microsoft Partner Network (MPN) portal, participate in training and certification programs to build their skills and expertise, and take advantage of marketing and go-to-market initiatives to promote their offerings and generate demand. Azure Marketplace and partnerships are critical components of Microsoft's strategy to drive *innovation and adoption in the cloud, offering customers a diverse ecosystem of solutions and services to address their evolving business needs and challenges. By leveraging the breadth and depth of offerings available on Azure Marketplace and collaborating with Microsoft and its partners, customers can accelerate their digital transformation journey, increase agility and scalability, and unlock new opportunities for growth and innovation in the cloud. Whether customers are looking for infrastructure solutions, applications, or services, Azure Marketplace and partnerships provide a rich and vibrant ecosystem of options to help them succeed in the cloud.*

Azure AI and Machine Learning Services empower organizations to harness the power of artificial intelligence and machine learning to drive innovation, efficiency, and business growth in the cloud. Azure offers a comprehensive suite of AI and machine learning services, tools, and frameworks that enable developers and data scientists to build, train, deploy, and manage intelligent applications and solutions at scale. One of the key services in the Azure AI portfolio is Azure Cognitive Services, which provides a set of pre-built AI models and APIs that enable developers to add cognitive capabilities such as vision, speech, language, and decision-making to their applications with minimal effort. With Azure Cognitive Services, developers can easily integrate features such as image recognition, text analysis, speech-to-text conversion, language translation, and sentiment analysis into their applications, enabling them to create more engaging and intelligent user experiences. Developers can use the Azure portal, Azure CLI, or Azure SDKs to provision and manage Cognitive Services resources, configure service settings, and integrate APIs into their applications using simple RESTful endpoints or SDKs for popular programming languages such as Python,

JavaScript, and .NET. Another key service in the Azure AI portfolio is Azure Machine Learning, which provides a cloud-based environment for building, training, and deploying machine learning models at scale. Azure Machine Learning enables data scientists and machine learning engineers to experiment with different algorithms, features, and parameters, and develop predictive models using a variety of tools and frameworks such as TensorFlow, PyTorch, and scikit-learn. Data scientists can use the Azure Machine Learning Studio to create and manage machine learning experiments, explore and visualize data, and train and evaluate models using automated machine learning capabilities. They can use the Azure CLI or Azure SDKs to interact with Azure Machine Learning workspaces, datasets, and experiments programmatically, enabling them to automate workflows and integrate machine learning into their DevOps pipelines. Azure Machine Learning also provides a range of deployment options, including Azure Kubernetes Service (AKS), Azure Container Instances (ACI), and Azure Functions, which enable organizations to deploy and scale machine learning models in production environments with ease. Additionally, Azure Machine Learning offers integration with Azure DevOps for model versioning, collaboration, and continuous integration and deployment (CI/CD), enabling teams to streamline the end-to-end machine learning lifecycle from development to deployment. Azure AI and Machine Learning Services also include specialized offerings such as Azure Bot Service, Azure Speech Service, Azure Vision Service, and Azure Language Understanding (LUIS), which enable organizations to build intelligent conversational agents, speech-enabled applications, computer vision solutions, and natural language processing (NLP) applications. For example, Azure Bot Service provides a platform for building, deploying, and managing conversational bots across multiple channels such as web, mobile, and messaging platforms, enabling organizations to automate customer service, support, and engagement workflows. Developers can use the Azure portal or the Bot Framework SDK to create and train bots, define conversation flows, and integrate with backend systems and APIs, enabling them to build sophisticated and personalized conversational experiences for their users. Similarly, Azure Speech Service provides a set of APIs for speech recognition, speech-to-text transcription, and text-to-speech synthesis, enabling developers to add speech capabilities to their applications and services. They can use the Azure portal or the Speech SDK to integrate speech recognition and synthesis into their applications, enabling users to interact with their applications using natural language and voice commands. Azure Vision Service *offers a set of APIs for image recognition, object detection, and image analysis, enabling developers to build computer vision solutions for a variety of use cases such as image classification, object detection, and facial recognition. Developers can use the Azure portal or the Computer Vision SDK to integrate vision capabilities into their applications, enabling them to analyze and extract insights from images and videos with ease. Azure Language Understanding (LUIS) is a natural language understanding service that enables developers to build language understanding models for conversational interfaces, chatbots, and virtual assistants. Developers can use the Azure portal or the LUIS SDK to define intents, entities, and utterances, and train and deploy language understanding models that can understand and interpret user input in natural language. In addition to pre-built services and APIs, Azure also offers a range of tools and frameworks for custom AI and machine learning development, including Azure Databricks, Azure Notebooks, and Azure HDInsight, which enable organizations to build and train custom machine learning models using popular frameworks such as TensorFlow, PyTorch, and Apache Spark. Data scientists and machine learning engineers can use Azure Databricks to create and run interactive notebooks, build and train machine learning models, and perform data processing and analysis at scale using Apache Spark. They can use Azure Notebooks to create and share Jupyter notebooks in the cloud, enabling collaboration and experimentation with data and code. They can use Azure HDInsight to deploy and manage Apache Hadoop, Spark, and HBase clusters in the cloud, enabling big data processing and analytics at scale. Overall, Azure AI and Machine Learning Services provide organizations with a powerful and flexible platform for building intelligent applications and solutions that leverage the latest advances in artificial intelligence and machine learning. By leveraging Azure AI and Machine Learning Services, organizations can unlock new opportunities for innovation, drive operational efficiency, and deliver better experiences for their customers and users.*

Azure IoT and Edge Computing Solutions represent a powerful suite of tools and services designed to empower organizations to build, deploy, and manage Internet of Things (IoT) solutions at scale, enabling them to connect, monitor, and control devices and sensors from anywhere in the world. Azure IoT Hub serves as the core of the Azure IoT platform, providing a scalable and secure cloud gateway for bi-directional communication between IoT devices and the cloud, allowing organizations to collect telemetry data, send commands, and implement device management capabilities at scale.

To create an IoT hub using the Azure CLI, you can use the az iot hub create command, specifying parameters such as resource group, name, and location. Once the IoT hub is created, you can configure device endpoints, access policies, and monitoring settings using the Azure portal or the Azure CLI. Azure IoT Edge extends the capabilities of Azure IoT to the edge of the network, enabling organizations to deploy and run IoT workloads and applications directly on edge devices, such as gateways and sensors, for low-latency processing and real-time decision-making. To deploy an IoT Edge device using the Azure CLI, you can use the az iot edge device create command, specifying parameters such as device ID and connection string. Once the device is provisioned, you can deploy modules to the device using the Azure portal or the Azure CLI, specifying Docker container images or Azure Function apps as the workload to be executed on the edge device. Azure IoT Central is a fully managed IoT platform-as-a-service (PaaS) offering that enables organizations to quickly and easily build, deploy, and manage IoT solutions without the need for complex infrastructure or expertise. To create an IoT Central application using the Azure CLI, you can use the az iot central app create command, specifying parameters such as name, SKU, and location. Once the application is created, you can configure devices, dashboards, rules, and alerts using the IoT Central web portal, enabling you to monitor and manage your IoT solution from anywhere in the world. Azure IoT Hub Device Provisioning Service (DPS) simplifies the process of provisioning and managing large numbers of IoT devices at scale, enabling organizations to enroll, authenticate, and provision devices automatically without manual intervention. To create a DPS instance using the Azure CLI, you can use the az iot dps create command, specifying parameters such as resource group, name, and location. Once the DPS instance is created, you can configure enrollment groups, individual enrollments, and attestation mechanisms using the Azure portal or the Azure CLI, enabling you to onboard devices securely and efficiently. Azure Stream Analytics is a real-time analytics service that enables organizations to ingest, process, and analyze streaming data from IoT devices and sensors in real-time, enabling them to derive insights and take action on the data as it arrives. To create a Stream Analytics job using the Azure CLI, you can use the az stream-analytics job create command, specifying parameters such as resource group, name, and location. Once the job is created, you can define input, output, and query configurations using the Azure portal or the Azure CLI, enabling you to process and analyze streaming data from IoT devices in real-time. Azure Time Series Insights is a fully managed analytics service that *enables organizations to explore and analyze time-series data from IoT devices and sensors at scale, enabling them to visualize trends, detect anomalies, and derive insights from their IoT data. To create a Time Series Insights environment using the Azure CLI, you can use the az timeseriesinsights environment create command, specifying parameters such as resource group, name, and location. Once the environment is created, you can configure event sources, data retention policies, and access control settings using the Azure portal or the Azure CLI, enabling you to ingest, store, and analyze time-series data from IoT devices and sensors. Azure IoT Edge modules are containers that encapsulate IoT workloads and applications, enabling organizations to deploy and run code directly on edge devices for local processing and analytics. To create an IoT Edge module using the Azure CLI, you can use the az iot hub module create command, specifying parameters such as module ID, Docker container image, and target device. Once the module is created, you can deploy it to an edge device using the Azure portal or the Azure CLI, enabling you to execute custom code and logic on the edge for real-time decision-making and data processing. Azure IoT Central offers a wide range of built-in features and capabilities, including device provisioning, device management, telemetry data ingestion, real-time monitoring, and analytics, enabling organizations to accelerate their IoT initiatives and bring solutions to market faster. By leveraging Azure IoT Central, organizations can reduce the complexity and cost of building and managing IoT solutions, enabling them to focus on innovation and delivering value to their customers. Azure IoT Hub Device Provisioning Service (DPS) provides a scalable and secure mechanism for enrolling and provisioning IoT devices at scale, enabling organizations to onboard devices quickly and efficiently without manual intervention. With Azure DPS, organizations can automate the device provisioning process, streamline device management workflows, and improve the security and reliability of their IoT deployments. Azure Stream Analytics enables organizations to process and analyze streaming data from IoT devices in real-time, enabling them to derive insights and take action on the data as it arrives. With Azure Stream Analytics, organizations can build and deploy complex event processing pipelines that ingest, transform, and analyze streaming data from a variety of sources, enabling them to monitor, detect, and respond to events and anomalies in real-time. Azure Time Series Insights provides organizations with a fully managed analytics service for exploring and analyzing time-series data from IoT devices and sensors at scale. With Azure Time Series Insights, organizations can visualize trends, detect*

Azure Active Directory (Azure AD) Basics and Identity Management are foundational aspects of any Azure deployment, serving as the cornerstone for securing access to Azure resources and managing user identities across the cloud. Azure AD provides a comprehensive identity and access management platform that enables organizations to authenticate and authorize users, devices, and applications, ensuring that only authorized entities can access resources and data in the Azure environment. To create an Azure Active Directory tenant using the Azure CLI, you can use the az ad tenant create command, specifying parameters such as tenant name and domain name. Once the Azure AD tenant is created, you can configure user accounts, groups, roles, and policies using the Azure portal or the Azure CLI, enabling you to define access controls and permissions for users and applications. Azure AD supports a variety of authentication methods, including passwords, multi-factor authentication (MFA), and single sign-on (SSO), enabling organizations to enforce strong authentication policies and protect against identity-related security threats. To enable multi-factor authentication for a user in Azure AD using the

Azure CLI, you can use the az ad user update command with the --add parameter to add a strongAuthenticationMethods property to the user object, specifying the desired authentication methods such as phone, email, or app notification. Once multi-factor authentication is enabled, users will be required to provide additional verification, such as a one-time passcode sent to their phone or email, when accessing Azure resources or applications. Azure AD also supports federated identity and single sign-on (SSO) capabilities, enabling organizations to integrate their on-premises Active Directory with Azure AD and provide users with seamless access to cloud resources and applications using their existing credentials. To configure single sign-on for an application in Azure AD using the Azure CLI, you can use the az ad app update command to update the application manifest, specifying the desired singleSignOnSettings such as saml or openidConnect, and providing the necessary configuration details such as the federation metadata URL or issuer URI. Once single sign-on is configured, users will be able to sign in to the application using their Azure AD credentials without having to enter their username and password separately. Azure AD also provides advanced identity protection capabilities, such as risk-based conditional access policies, identity protection reports, and anomaly detection algorithms, enabling organizations to detect and mitigate identity-related security risks in real-time. To create a conditional access policy in Azure AD using the Azure CLI, you can use the az ad policy assignment create command, specifying parameters such as policy type, conditions, and actions. Once the policy is created, it will be automatically applied to users and devices based on the defined criteria, enabling organizations to enforce access controls and security policies based on risk levels and user behavior. Azure AD Identity Protection provides organizations with insights and recommendations for securing user identities and detecting suspicious activities, enabling them to take proactive measures to protect against identity-related security threats. To enable Identity Protection for Azure AD using the Azure CLI, you can use the az ad identity-protection update command, specifying parameters such as isEnabled and notifyOnNewRiskEvent, and providing the necessary configuration details such as riskDetectionLevel and riskThreshold, to enable risk-based authentication and notification settings. Once Identity Protection is enabled, organizations can leverage the built-in risk detection algorithms and machine learning models to identify and remediate potential security risks, such as compromised accounts, suspicious sign-in activities, and risky authentication attempts. Azure AD also provides organizations with comprehensive identity governance capabilities, including privileged identity management (PIM), access reviews, and entitlement management, enabling them to enforce least privilege access controls and ensure compliance with regulatory requirements. To enable privileged identity management for Azure AD using the Azure CLI, you can use the az ad pim update command, specifying parameters such as isEnabled and isMfaActivated, and providing the necessary configuration details such as eligibleRoles and activationDurationInDays, to enable just-in-time access and multi-factor authentication for privileged roles. Once privileged identity management is enabled, organizations can enforce access controls and approval workflows for privileged roles, ensuring that users only have access to resources and data that are necessary for their job responsibilities. Azure AD also supports access reviews, which enable organizations to periodically review and recertify user access to resources and applications, enabling them to identify and remove stale or unnecessary permissions. To create an access review in Azure AD using the Azure CLI, you can use the az ad accessreview command, specifying parameters such as targetResource and reviewers, and providing the necessary configuration details such as reviewers' email addresses and review duration. Once the access review is created, reviewers will be notified to review and recertify user access, and administrators can track the progress and results of the review using the Azure portal or the Azure CLI. Overall, Azure AD Basics and Identity Management are critical components of any Azure deployment, providing organizations with the tools and capabilities they need to secure access to resources, protect user identities, and ensure compliance with regulatory requirements. By leveraging Azure AD, organizations can enforce strong authentication policies, enable seamless single sign-on experiences, and protect against identity-related security threats, enabling them to build and maintain a secure and compliant cloud environment.

Advanced Azure AD Configurations and Integrations delve into sophisticated techniques for optimizing Azure Active Directory (Azure AD) deployments and seamlessly integrating with other Azure services and third-party applications. Azure AD B2B (Business-to-Business) collaboration facilitates secure cross-organization collaboration by allowing external users to access resources and applications in your Azure AD tenant. To configure Azure AD B2B settings, administrators can navigate to the Azure portal, select Azure Active Directory, and then select External Identities to configure settings such as invitation settings, authentication methods, and user attributes. Azure AD B2C (Business-to-

Consumer) enables organizations to build customer-facing applications and authenticate external users using social identity providers such as Microsoft, Google, Facebook, and Twitter. Administrators can configure Azure AD B2C policies, user flows, and identity providers using the Azure portal or programmatically using Azure CLI commands such as az ad b2c policy create and az ad b2c identity-provider facebook create. Conditional Access policies enable organizations to enforce access controls based on user and device conditions, risk levels, and session controls, ensuring that only authorized users can access resources and applications under predefined conditions. Administrators can create and manage Conditional Access policies using the Azure portal or the Azure CLI, specifying conditions, assignments, and access controls using commands such as az ad conditional-access policy create and az ad conditional-access policy assignment create. Azure AD Privileged Identity Management (PIM) enables organizations to manage and monitor access to privileged roles in Azure AD, Azure, and other Microsoft Online Services, reducing the risk of unauthorized access and data breaches. Administrators can enable Azure AD PIM using the Azure portal or the Azure CLI, assigning eligible roles, activation settings, and access reviews using commands such as az ad pim role assignment create and az ad pim role definition *list. Azure AD Connect is a tool that enables organizations to synchronize on-premises Active Directory with Azure AD, ensuring that user accounts, passwords, and group memberships are kept in sync across both environments. Administrators can install and configure Azure AD Connect using the Azure portal or the Azure CLI, specifying options such as express settings or custom settings using commands such as az ad connect sync. Azure AD Domain Services provides managed domain services such as domain join, group policy, LDAP, and Kerberos authentication, enabling organizations to lift-and-shift legacy applications to Azure without the need for domain controllers. Administrators can enable Azure AD Domain Services using the Azure portal or the Azure CLI, specifying options such as domain name, subnet, and virtual network using commands such as az ad ds create. Azure AD Application Proxy enables organizations to securely publish on-premises web applications to external users without exposing them to the internet, providing secure remote access and single sign-on capabilities. Administrators can configure Azure AD Application Proxy using the Azure portal or the Azure CLI, adding applications, configuring settings, and assigning users using commands such as az ad app proxy create and az ad app proxy app update. Azure AD Multi-Factor Authentication (MFA) provides an additional layer of security by requiring users to provide two or more forms of verification before accessing resources and applications, reducing the risk of unauthorized access and data breaches. Administrators can enable Azure AD MFA using the Azure portal or the Azure CLI, configuring settings such as authentication methods, verification options, and user assignments using commands such as az ad user mfa update. Azure AD Security Defaults are pre-configured security settings that help organizations protect against common identity-related attacks such as password spray attacks, replay attacks, and phishing attacks, reducing the risk of unauthorized access and data breaches. Administrators can enable Azure AD Security Defaults using the Azure portal or the Azure CLI, specifying options such as user assignments and enforcement settings using commands such as az ad security identity-protection update. Azure AD Identity Protection provides organizations with insights and recommendations for securing user identities and detecting suspicious activities, enabling them to take proactive measures to protect against identity-related security threats. Administrators can enable Azure AD Identity Protection using the Azure portal or the Azure CLI, configuring settings such as risk detection policies, user notifications, and risk remediation using commands such as az ad identity-protection update.*

Azure AD Reporting and Monitoring provide organizations with visibility into user sign-in activities, authentication methods, and security events, enabling them to monitor and analyze user behavior and detect anomalous activities. Administrators can access Azure AD reports and logs using the Azure portal or programmatically using the Azure CLI, querying sign-in logs, audit logs, and security alerts using commands such as az monitor activity-log list. Overall, Advanced Azure AD Configurations and Integrations empower organizations to enhance security, streamline access controls, and improve user productivity by leveraging advanced features and capabilities of Azure Active Directory. By mastering these techniques, organizations can build robust identity and access management solutions that meet their unique business requirements and compliance needs.

Creating and Managing Azure Virtual Machines (VMs) is a fundamental skill for anyone working with Azure infrastructure, offering flexibility, scalability, and control over computing resources in the cloud environment. To create a virtual machine in Azure using the Azure portal, you can navigate to the Virtual Machines section, click on the "Add" button, and then follow the guided steps to configure the VM settings, such as name, region, size, operating system, and authentication method. Alternatively, you can deploy a VM using the Azure CLI by running the az vm create command, specifying parameters such as resource group, name, image, size, and authentication type. Once the VM is created, you can connect to it using Remote Desktop Protocol (RDP) for Windows VMs or Secure Shell (SSH) for Linux VMs, enabling you to configure and manage the VM remotely. Azure VM Scale Sets enable organizations to deploy and manage a group of identical VMs that automatically scale in and out based on demand or a predefined schedule, ensuring high availability and performance for applications and services. To create a VM scale set in Azure using the Azure portal, you can navigate to the Virtual Machine Scale Sets section, click on the "Add" button, and then follow the guided steps to configure the scale set settings, such as name, region, capacity, and scaling options. Alternatively, you can deploy a VM scale set using the Azure CLI by running the az vmss create command, specifying parameters such as resource group, name, image, capacity, and scaling rules. Once the scale set is created, Azure will automatically manage the scaling of VM instances based on the configured rules, ensuring optimal performance and cost efficiency. Azure VM Extensions are software components that enable organizations to customize and configure VMs with additional features and capabilities, such as monitoring agents, antivirus software, and custom scripts. To deploy a VM extension in Azure using the Azure portal, you can navigate to the Extensions section of the VM settings, click on the "Add" button, and then select the desired extension from the marketplace or provide a custom script or configuration file. Alternatively, you can install a VM extension using the Azure CLI by running the az vm extension set command, specifying parameters such as resource group, VM name, extension type, and settings. Once the extension is deployed, it will be automatically installed and configured on the VM, enabling you to enhance its functionality and manageability. Azure VM Backup enables organizations to protect and recover data from Azure VMs by creating backup copies of VM disks and storing them in a secure and scalable manner, ensuring data resilience and compliance with regulatory requirements. To enable VM backup in Azure using the Azure portal, you can navigate to the Backup section of the VM settings, click on the "Backup" button, and then follow the guided steps to configure the backup policy, retention settings, and backup vault. Alternatively, you can configure VM backup using the Azure CLI by running the az backup protect command, specifying parameters such as resource group, VM name, backup policy, and retention period. Once the backup is configured, Azure will automatically create backup copies of VM disks according to the specified policy, enabling you to restore data from any point in time in case of data loss or corruption. Azure VM Auto-Shutdown enables organizations to save costs and improve resource utilization by automatically shutting down VMs during non-business hours or periods of low usage, reducing the consumption of compute resources and minimizing unnecessary spending. To configure auto-shutdown for a VM in Azure using the Azure portal, you can navigate to the Auto-shutdown section of the VM settings, click on the "Enable" button, and then specify the shutdown schedule and notification preferences. Alternatively, you can configure auto-shutdown using the Azure

CLI by running the az vm auto-shutdown set command, specifying parameters such as resource group, VM name, and shutdown time. Once auto-shutdown is enabled, Azure will automatically shut down the VM at the specified time, enabling you to save costs and optimize resource usage without manual intervention. Azure VM Monitoring enables organizations to monitor the performance and health of VMs in real-time, enabling them to identify and troubleshoot issues proactively, optimize resource utilization, and ensure high availability and performance for applications and services. To enable VM monitoring in Azure using the Azure portal, you can navigate to the Monitoring section of the VM settings, click on the "Enable" button, and then follow the guided steps to configure monitoring settings such as metrics, logs, and alerts. Alternatively, you can configure VM monitoring using the Azure CLI by running the az monitor diagnostic-settings create command, specifying parameters such as resource group, VM name, diagnostic settings, and storage account. Once monitoring is enabled, Azure will collect performance metrics and logs from the VM and provide insights and alerts based on predefined thresholds and conditions, enabling you to monitor and optimize the performance and health of your VMs effectively. Overall, Creating and Managing Azure VMs are essential skills for cloud administrators and developers, enabling them to deploy, customize, and optimize virtualized infrastructure in the Azure environment efficiently. By mastering these techniques, organizations can leverage the full potential of Azure VMs to build scalable, resilient, and cost-effective solutions that meet their business needs and objectives. Scaling and Load Balancing with Azure Scale Sets are essential strategies for ensuring high availability, scalability, and performance of applications and services in the Azure cloud environment. Azure Virtual Machine Scale Sets enable organizations to deploy and manage a group of identical VMs that automatically scale in and out based on demand or a predefined schedule, ensuring that applications can handle increased workloads and traffic without manual intervention. To create a VM scale set in Azure, administrators can use the Azure portal or the Azure CLI, specifying parameters such as resource group, name, image, capacity, and scaling options. Once the scale set is created, Azure will automatically manage the scaling of VM instances based on the configured rules, ensuring optimal performance and cost efficiency. Azure Load Balancer is a network load balancer service that distributes incoming traffic across multiple VM instances within a scale set, enabling organizations to achieve high availability, fault tolerance, and scalability for their applications.

To configure a load balancer for a VM scale set in Azure, administrators can use the Azure portal or the Azure CLI, specifying parameters such as frontend IP configuration, backend pool, health probe, and load balancing rules. Once the load balancer is configured, it will distribute incoming traffic evenly across the VM instances in the scale set, ensuring that each instance receives its fair share of requests and can handle the workload effectively. Azure Application Gateway is a layer 7 load balancer service that provides advanced traffic management capabilities such as SSL termination, URL-based routing, session affinity, and web application firewall (WAF), enabling organizations to optimize performance, security, and availability for their web applications. To configure an application gateway for a VM scale set in Azure, administrators can use the Azure portal or the Azure CLI, specifying parameters such as frontend IP configuration, backend pool, HTTP settings, and routing rules. Once the application gateway is configured, it will intelligently route incoming traffic to the appropriate VM instances based on the defined routing rules and policies, ensuring efficient and secure delivery of web applications to end users. Autoscaling is a feature of Azure Virtual Machine Scale Sets that automatically adjusts the number of VM instances in the scale set based on predefined scaling rules and metrics such as CPU utilization, memory usage, and network traffic, enabling organizations to optimize resource utilization and minimize costs. To configure autoscaling for a VM scale set in Azure, administrators can use the Azure portal or the Azure CLI, specifying parameters such as scaling rules, metrics, and thresholds. Once autoscaling is enabled, Azure will automatically add or remove VM instances from the scale set based on the current workload and resource utilization, ensuring that applications can dynamically scale to meet demand without overprovisioning or underprovisioning resources. Azure Monitor is a comprehensive monitoring and management service that enables organizations to monitor the performance, health, and availability of their Azure resources and applications, including VM scale sets. To monitor a VM scale set in Azure, administrators can use Azure Monitor to collect and analyze performance metrics, logs, and alerts from the VM instances in the scale set, enabling them to identify and troubleshoot issues proactively, optimize resource utilization, and ensure high availability and performance for their applications and services. Azure Advisor is a personalized recommendation engine that provides best practices and optimization recommendations for Azure resources, including VM scale sets, based on usage patterns, performance metrics, and industry standards. To optimize a VM scale set in Azure, administrators can use Azure

Advisor to review and implement recommendations such as right-sizing VM instances, optimizing scaling rules, configuring health probes, and enabling autoscaling, enabling them to improve the performance, efficiency, and cost-effectiveness of their applications and services. Overall, Scaling and Load Balancing with Azure Scale Sets are critical techniques for achieving high availability, scalability, and performance for applications and services in the Azure cloud environment. By leveraging features such as VM scale sets, load balancers, autoscaling, monitoring, and optimization tools, organizations can build resilient, efficient, and cost-effective solutions that meet their business needs and objectives.

Azure Blob Storage is a fundamental component of the Azure cloud platform, providing scalable, durable, and cost-effective storage solutions for a wide range of data types, including documents, images, videos, logs, and backups. To create a storage account in Azure using the Azure portal, administrators can navigate to the Storage Accounts section, click on the "Add" button, and then follow the guided steps to configure the storage account settings, such as name, region, performance, and redundancy options. Alternatively, you can create a storage account using the Azure CLI by running the az storage account create command, specifying parameters such as resource group, name, location, and SKU. Once the storage account is created, you can create Blob containers to organize and manage your data within the storage account. To create a Blob container in Azure using the Azure portal, you can navigate to the Blob service section of the storage account, click on the "Containers" tab, and then click on the "New container" button to specify the container name, access level, and metadata. Alternatively, you can create a Blob container using the Azure CLI by running the az storage container create command, specifying parameters such as storage account name and container name. Once the Blob container is created, you can upload Blob data to the container using various methods such as the Azure portal, Azure Storage Explorer, or programmatically using the Azure SDKs or REST API. To upload Blob data to a container using the Azure portal, you can navigate to the Blob container, click on the "Upload" button, and then select the files or folders you want to upload from your local machine. Alternatively, you can upload Blob data using the Azure CLI by running the az storage blob upload command, specifying parameters such as storage account name, container name, local file path, and Blob name. Once the Blob data is uploaded to the container, you can manage it using various features and capabilities provided by Azure Blob Storage. For example, you can set Blob properties such as metadata, access tier, and content type, configure Blob lifecycle management policies to automatically move or delete Blob data based on predefined rules, enable versioning to maintain a history of Blob changes and revisions, and implement data encryption at rest using Azure Storage Service Encryption (SSE) or customer-managed keys (CMK). Additionally, you can monitor and analyze Blob storage usage, performance, and activity using Azure Monitor metrics, logs, and alerts, enabling you to identify and troubleshoot issues, optimize resource utilization, and ensure compliance with regulatory requirements. Azure Blob Storage also integrates with other Azure services and solutions, enabling organizations to build scalable and resilient data-driven applications and workflows. For example, you can use Azure Functions to trigger serverless functions in response to Blob storage events such as Blob creation, update, or deletion, enabling you to automate business processes, data processing tasks, and data integration workflows. Similarly, you can use Azure Data Factory to orchestrate and automate data movement and transformation tasks between Blob storage and other data sources such as SQL databases, data lakes, and cloud applications, enabling you to build modern data pipelines and analytics solutions. Overall, Azure Blob Storage provides a versatile and scalable platform for storing and managing data in the cloud, enabling organizations to leverage the full potential of their data to drive innovation, insight, and business value. By understanding the fundamentals of Azure Blob Storage and mastering its features and capabilities, organizations can build robust and scalable data storage solutions that meet their evolving business needs and objectives. Azure File and Queue Storage Solutions are essential components of the Azure cloud platform, offering scalable, secure, and highly available storage solutions for various application scenarios. Azure File Storage provides fully managed file shares in the cloud that can be accessed via the industry-standard Server Message Block (SMB) protocol, enabling organizations to share files across Windows, Linux, and macOS environments seamlessly. To create an Azure File Share using the Azure portal, administrators can navigate to the Storage Accounts section, click on the "Add" button, and then follow the guided steps to configure the storage account settings, such as name, region, performance, and redundancy options. Alternatively, you can create an Azure File Share using the Azure CLI by running the az storage share create command, specifying parameters such as storage account name and share name. Once the file share is created, you can mount it as a network drive on your local machine or access it programmatically using the Azure Storage SDKs or REST API. Azure File Storage supports various features such as access control, encryption, snapshots, and Azure Active Directory integration, enabling organizations to secure and manage their file shares effectively. Azure Queue Storage provides a scalable message queuing service in the cloud that enables decoupled and asynchronous communication between application components, enabling organizations to build scalable and resilient distributed systems. To create an Azure Queue using the Azure portal, administrators can navigate to the Storage Accounts section, click on the "Add" button, and then follow the guided steps to configure the storage account settings, such as name, region, performance, and redundancy options. Alternatively, you can create an Azure Queue using the Azure CLI by running the az storage queue create command, specifying parameters such as storage account name and queue name. Once the queue is created, you can enqueue and dequeue messages from it using various methods such as the Azure portal, Azure Storage Explorer, or programmatically using the Azure SDKs or REST API. Azure Queue Storage supports features such as message expiration, visibility timeout, and message batching, enabling organizations to build reliable and scalable message-based communication patterns in their applications. Azure File and Queue Storage Solutions integrate seamlessly with other Azure services and solutions, enabling organizations to build scalable and resilient cloud-native applications and workflows. For example, you can use Azure Functions to process messages from Azure Queue Storage and trigger serverless functions in response to message events, enabling you to automate business processes, data processing tasks, and application workflows. Similarly, you can use Azure Logic Apps to orchestrate and automate workflows that involve Azure File Storage, enabling you to integrate file-based data processing tasks with other Azure services and external systems. Azure File and

Queue Storage Solutions also provide advanced features such as Azure AD authentication, role-based access control (RBAC), and data encryption at rest, enabling organizations to meet their security and compliance requirements effectively. Additionally, Azure File Storage supports features such as Azure File Sync, which enables organizations to synchronize on-premises file servers with Azure File Shares, enabling centralized file management, collaboration, and disaster recovery. Azure Queue Storage supports features such as message logging and monitoring, which enable organizations to monitor queue activity, track message processing times, and troubleshoot issues effectively. Overall, Azure File and Queue Storage Solutions are essential components of the Azure cloud platform, enabling organizations to build scalable, secure, and highly available storage solutions for various application scenarios. By understanding the fundamentals of Azure File and Queue Storage and mastering their features and capabilities, organizations can leverage the full potential of Azure storage services to drive innovation, efficiency, and business value.

Azure Virtual Network (VNet) Essentials are foundational for building secure and isolated network environments in the Azure cloud, providing organizations with the flexibility to design and manage their own private networks with control over IP address ranges, subnets, routing, and security policies. To create a virtual network in Azure using the Azure portal, administrators can navigate to the Virtual Networks section, click on the "Add" button, and then follow the guided steps to configure the VNet settings, such as name, region, address space, and subnets. Alternatively, you can create a virtual network using the Azure CLI by running the az network vnet create command, specifying parameters such as resource group, name, location, and address prefixes. Once the virtual network is created, you can create subnets within the VNet to segment your network resources and define routing and security policies to control traffic flow between subnets and to and from on-premises networks or other VNets. Azure Virtual Network Peering enables organizations to establish private, low-latency connections between VNets in the same region or different regions, enabling seamless communication between resources deployed in different VNets without the need for gateways or public internet access. To create a virtual network peering in Azure using the Azure portal, administrators can navigate to the Virtual Network Peering section of the VNet settings, click on the "Add" button, and then follow the guided steps to configure the peering settings, such as remote VNet, peering type, and traffic forwarding options. Alternatively, you can create a virtual network peering using the Azure CLI by running the az network vnet peering create command, specifying parameters such as resource group, VNet name, remote VNet name, and peering options. Once the peering is established, resources in the peered VNets can communicate with each other using private IP addresses, enabling organizations to build distributed applications and services that span multiple VNets and regions while maintaining network isolation and security. Azure Virtual Network Gateway enables organizations to establish secure, encrypted connections between their Azure VNets and on-premises networks or other VNets in Azure, enabling seamless connectivity and data transfer between resources deployed in different environments. To create a virtual network gateway in Azure using the Azure portal, administrators can navigate to the Virtual Network Gateway section, click on the "Add" button, and then follow the guided steps to configure the gateway settings, such as name, region, gateway type, and SKU. Alternatively, you can create a virtual network gateway using the Azure CLI by running the az network vnet-gateway create command, specifying parameters such as resource group, gateway name, VPN type, and SKU. Once the gateway is created, you can configure connections such as site-to-site VPN, point-to-site VPN, or ExpressRoute to establish connectivity between your Azure VNets and on-premises networks or other VNets in Azure. Azure ExpressRoute enables organizations to establish private, dedicated connections to Azure data centers through a network service provider, enabling predictable performance, low latency, and high security for mission-critical workloads and data transfer. To create an ExpressRoute circuit in Azure using the Azure portal, administrators can navigate to the ExpressRoute Circuits section, click on the "Create" button, and then follow the guided steps to configure the circuit settings, such as name, region, bandwidth, and peering locations. Alternatively, you can create an ExpressRoute circuit using the Azure CLI by running the az network express-route create command, specifying parameters such as resource group, circuit name, bandwidth, and peering locations. Once the circuit is provisioned, you can configure peering with your Azure VNets and on-premises networks to establish private, dedicated connections for data transfer and access to Azure services. Azure Virtual Network Essentials also include features such as Network Security Groups (NSGs), which enable organizations to define granular network security policies and control inbound and outbound traffic to and from Azure resources based on source and destination IP addresses, ports, and protocols. To create a Network Security Group in Azure using the Azure portal, administrators can navigate to the Network Security Groups section, click on the "Add" button, and then follow the guided steps to configure the NSG settings, such as name, region, and security rules. Alternatively, you can create a Network Security Group using the Azure CLI by running the az network nsg create command, specifying parameters such as resource group and name. Once the NSG is created, you can associate it with your Azure VNets and subnets to enforce security policies and control traffic flow within your virtual network environment. Overall, Azure Virtual Network Essentials provide organizations with the foundational building blocks for designing and implementing secure, scalable, and highly available network architectures in the Azure cloud, enabling them to connect, isolate, and protect their resources effectively while optimizing performance and minimizing costs. By understanding the core concepts and features of Azure Virtual Networks and mastering their deployment and configuration techniques, organizations can build robust and resilient network infrastructures that meet their business needs and objectives. Azure VPN and ExpressRoute Connectivity Options provide organizations with flexible and reliable connectivity solutions to connect their on-premises networks, branch offices, and data centers to Azure, enabling seamless integration and access to cloud resources securely. Azure VPN Gateway is a fully managed virtual network gateway service that enables organizations to establish encrypted VPN tunnels between their on-premises networks and Azure VNets, providing secure and private communication over the public internet. To create a VPN gateway in Azure using the Azure portal, administrators can navigate to the VPN Gateway section, click on the "Create" button, and then follow the guided steps to configure the gateway settings, such as name, region, VPN type, and SKU. Alternatively, you can create a VPN gateway using the Azure CLI by running the az network vpn-gateway create command, specifying parameters such as resource group, gateway name, VPN type, and SKU. Once the VPN gateway is provisioned, you can configure connections such as site-to-site VPN or point-to-site VPN to establish connectivity between your on-premises networks and Azure

VNets. Site-to-site VPN enables organizations to connect their on-premises networks to Azure VNets securely through encrypted VPN tunnels over the public internet, enabling seamless access to Azure resources and services. To configure site-to-site VPN connectivity in Azure, administrators can configure VPN settings such as local network gateway, connection type, shared key, and routing options, enabling them to establish secure and reliable connectivity between their on-premises networks and Azure VNets. Alternatively, you can configure site-to-site VPN connectivity using the Azure CLI by running the *az network vpn-connection create* command, specifying parameters such as VPN gateway, local network gateway, and connection type. Once the VPN connection is established, traffic between on-premises networks and Azure VNets will be encrypted and transmitted securely over the VPN tunnels, enabling organizations to extend their on-premises networks to Azure seamlessly. Point-to-site VPN enables individual users or devices to connect securely to Azure VNets from remote locations or mobile devices through encrypted VPN tunnels over the public internet, enabling remote access to Azure resources and services. To configure point-to-site VPN connectivity in Azure, administrators can configure VPN settings such as address pool, authentication type, and VPN client configuration, enabling them to establish secure and convenient *connectivity for remote users and devices. Alternatively, you can configure point-to-site VPN connectivity using the Azure CLI by running the az network vpn-client create command, specifying parameters such as VPN gateway, address pool, authentication type, and VPN client configuration. Once the point-to-site VPN connection is established, remote users and devices can connect securely to Azure VNets and access resources and services as if they were on-premises, enabling organizations to enable remote work and mobile access effectively. ExpressRoute is a private, dedicated connection service that enables organizations to establish high-speed, low-latency connections to Azure data centers through a network service provider, enabling predictable performance, reliability, and security for mission-critical workloads and data transfer. To create an ExpressRoute circuit in Azure using the Azure portal, administrators can navigate to the ExpressRoute Circuits section, click on the "Create" button, and then follow the guided steps to configure the circuit settings, such as name, region, bandwidth, and peering locations. Alternatively, you can create an ExpressRoute circuit using the Azure CLI by running the az network express-route create command, specifying parameters such as resource group, circuit name, bandwidth, and peering locations. Once the circuit is provisioned, you can configure peering with your on-premises networks and Azure VNets to establish private, dedicated connections for data transfer and access to Azure services. ExpressRoute Direct is a premium ExpressRoute offering that provides dedicated, high-bandwidth connections to Azure data centers through a network service provider, enabling organizations to achieve even higher levels of performance, scalability, and reliability for their mission-critical workloads and data transfer. To create an ExpressRoute Direct circuit in Azure using the Azure portal, administrators can navigate to the ExpressRoute Direct section, click on the "Create" button, and then follow the guided steps to configure the circuit settings, such as name, region, bandwidth, and peering locations. Alternatively, you can create an ExpressRoute Direct circuit using the Azure CLI by running the az network express-route create command, specifying parameters such as resource group, circuit name, bandwidth, and peering locations. Once the ExpressRoute Direct circuit is provisioned, you can configure peering with your on-premises networks and Azure VNets to establish dedicated, high-bandwidth connections for data transfer and access to Azure services. Overall, Azure VPN and ExpressRoute Connectivity Options provide organizations with flexible and reliable connectivity solutions to connect their on-premises networks, branch offices, and data centers to Azure,* enabling seamless integration and access to cloud resources securely. By understanding the core concepts and features of Azure VPN and ExpressRoute and mastering their deployment and configuration techniques, organizations can build robust and resilient network infrastructures that meet their business needs and objectives effectively.

Azure Security Center is a comprehensive cloud security management service provided by Microsoft Azure, designed to help organizations prevent, detect, and respond to security threats across their Azure resources. Azure Security Center continuously monitors the security posture of Azure resources, providing organizations with actionable insights and recommendations to improve their security posture and protect against evolving threats. To enable Azure Security Center for a subscription in the Azure portal, administrators can navigate to the Security Center section, click on the "Enable" button, and then follow the guided steps to configure the security settings, such as pricing tier, workspace settings, and data collection options. Alternatively, you can enable Azure Security Center using the Azure CLI by running the az security pricing create command, specifying parameters such as resource group, pricing tier, and workspace settings. Once Azure Security Center is enabled, it starts analyzing the security state of Azure resources, identifying potential security vulnerabilities, misconfigurations, and threats across the subscription. Azure Security Center provides a centralized dashboard that displays security recommendations, alerts, and compliance status, enabling organizations to prioritize and remediate security issues effectively. The Secure Score feature in Azure Security Center helps organizations measure and improve their security posture by providing a numerical score based on the implementation of security best practices and recommendations. To view the Secure Score in Azure Security Center, administrators can navigate to the Secure Score section of the dashboard, which provides a breakdown of security recommendations and their impact on the overall score. Azure Security Center integrates with Azure Policy to enforce compliance with regulatory standards and industry best practices by defining and applying security policies across Azure resources. Administrators can create custom policies in Azure Security Center to enforce specific security configurations and settings, such as network security groups, encryption, access controls, and software updates. To create a custom policy in Azure Security Center, administrators can navigate to the Policies section, click on the "Create Policy" button, and then follow the guided steps to define the policy settings, such as name, description, scope, and *evaluation criteria. Azure Security Center continuously evaluates resources against defined policies, generating compliance reports and recommendations to help organizations maintain a secure and compliant environment. Azure Security Center provides advanced threat detection capabilities to help organizations identify and respond to security threats proactively. The Threat Detection feature in Azure Security Center analyzes telemetry data from Azure resources, such as virtual machines, databases, and applications, to detect suspicious activities and indicators of compromise (IoCs). To configure threat detection in Azure Security Center, administrators can navigate to the Threat Detection section, select the resources to monitor, and then enable threat detection settings such as baseline policies, anomaly detection, and behavioral analytics. Azure Security Center generates security alerts for detected threats, providing detailed information about the alert severity, impacted resources, and recommended actions for mitigation. Azure Security Center also integrates with Azure Sentinel, Microsoft's cloud-native security information and event management (SIEM) service, to enable organizations to correlate security events and alerts from across their Azure environment and other sources for comprehensive threat detection and response. Azure Security Center provides built-in threat intelligence feeds and security recommendations curated by Microsoft's cybersecurity experts to help organizations stay ahead of emerging threats and vulnerabilities. Administrators can configure security alerts in Azure Security Center to trigger automated response actions, such as sending notifications, blocking suspicious IP addresses, quarantining compromised resources, or launching investigation workflows. Azure Security Center also supports integration with third-party security solutions and tools through its extensible APIs and integration frameworks, enabling organizations to leverage their existing investments in security technologies and workflows. Overall, Azure Security Center is a powerful cloud security management service that provides organizations with comprehensive visibility, control, and protection across their Azure resources. By leveraging the features and capabilities of Azure Security Center, organizations can strengthen their security posture, mitigate risks, and safeguard their cloud workloads and data effectively.*

Implementing Azure Resource Policies and Security Controls is crucial for organizations to enforce governance, compliance, and security standards across their Azure environments. Azure Policy is a service in Azure that allows organizations to create, assign, and manage policies to enforce rules and regulations on resources deployed in Azure. To create a new policy in Azure Policy using the Azure portal, administrators can navigate to the Policy Definitions section, click on the "Add policy definition" button, and then follow the guided steps to define the policy settings, such as name, description, and rules. Alternatively, you can create a policy definition using the Azure CLI by running the az policy definition create command, specifying parameters such as name, display name, description, and rule JSON. Once the policy definition is created, administrators can assign it to specific scopes, such as management groups, subscriptions, or resource groups, to enforce compliance with the defined rules. Azure Policy provides a wide range of built-in policy definitions covering common regulatory standards, industry best practices, and Azure resource types, such as virtual machines, storage accounts, and networking resources. Organizations can also create custom policy definitions tailored to their specific requirements and compliance needs using Azure Policy's flexible rule language and template options. To assign a policy to a specific scope in Azure Policy using the

Azure portal, administrators can navigate to the Assignments section, click on the "Assign policy" button, and then follow the guided steps to select the policy definition, scope, and parameters. Alternatively, you can assign a policy using the Azure CLI by running the az policy assignment create command, specifying parameters such as name, policy, scope, and parameters JSON. Once the policy assignment is created, Azure Policy evaluates resources within the assigned scope and enforces the defined rules and regulations, generating compliance reports and recommendations to help organizations maintain a secure and compliant environment. Azure Policy integrates with Azure Resource Manager to enforce policy compliance during resource deployment and management operations, such as resource creation, updates, and deletions. When a resource operation is initiated in Azure, Azure Resource Manager evaluates the associated policies and enforces any applicable rules or regulations before completing the operation. If a resource violates a policy, Azure Resource Manager prevents the operation from proceeding and provides feedback to the user about the policy violation. Azure Policy also supports remediation tasks to automatically correct non-compliant resources and bring them into compliance with the defined rules. To enable remediation tasks for a policy in Azure Policy using the Azure portal, administrators can navigate to the Remediation tasks section, click on the "Add remediation" button, and then follow the guided steps to configure the remediation task settings, such as name, description, and parameters. Alternatively, you can enable remediation tasks using the Azure CLI by running the az policy remediation create command, specifying parameters such as name, policy assignment, and resource scope. Once the remediation task is enabled, Azure Policy automatically scans for non-compliant resources and triggers remediation actions to bring them into compliance, such as modifying resource configurations or deploying additional resources. Azure Policy integrates with Azure Security Center to provide organizations with a unified view of their compliance and security posture across Azure resources. Administrators can configure security policies in Azure Security Center to enforce regulatory standards, industry best practices, and security controls, and then monitor compliance with these policies using Azure Policy. Azure Policy also integrates with Azure DevOps to enable organizations to enforce policy compliance during the development and deployment of infrastructure as code (IaC) templates and resource *configurations. By integrating Azure Policy into their CI/CD pipelines, organizations can enforce governance and security standards throughout the entire lifecycle of their Azure resources, ensuring consistency, reliability, and compliance across all deployments. Overall, implementing Azure Resource Policies and Security Controls is essential for organizations to enforce governance, compliance, and security standards across their Azure environments effectively. By leveraging the features and capabilities of Azure Policy, organizations can define and enforce rules and regulations to govern resource configurations, access controls, and compliance requirements, enabling them to maintain a secure and compliant cloud environment that meets their business needs and objectives.*

Azure Monitor and Insights Tools are essential components of Microsoft Azure's ecosystem, providing organizations with comprehensive visibility, monitoring, and analytics capabilities to optimize the performance, availability, and security of their cloud workloads. Azure Monitor is a centralized monitoring service that helps organizations collect, analyze, and act on telemetry data from Azure resources, applications, and infrastructure. To enable Azure Monitor for a subscription in the Azure portal, administrators can navigate to the Monitor section, click on the "Insights (preview)" tab, and then follow the guided steps to enable the monitoring settings, such as data collection, storage, and retention. Alternatively, you can enable Azure Monitor using the Azure CLI by running the az monitor diagnostic-settings create command, specifying parameters such as resource group, resource type, resource name, and diagnostics settings. Once Azure Monitor is enabled, it starts collecting telemetry data from Azure resources, such as virtual machines, databases, and applications, providing organizations with real-time insights into their performance, health, and usage. Azure Monitor supports a wide range of data sources and telemetry types, including logs, metrics, traces, and events, enabling organizations to monitor and analyze diverse aspects of their cloud environment effectively. Azure Monitor integrates with Azure Log Analytics to provide organizations with advanced log management and analytics capabilities, enabling them to collect, correlate, and analyze log data from Azure resources and applications centrally. To configure log analytics in Azure Monitor using the Azure portal, administrators can navigate to the Log Analytics section, click on the "Create workspace" button, and then follow the guided steps to configure the workspace settings, such as name, region, pricing tier, and data retention. Alternatively, you can create a log analytics workspace using the Azure CLI by running the az monitor log-analytics workspace create command, specifying parameters such as resource group, workspace name, region, and pricing tier. Once the log analytics workspace is created, organizations can start ingesting log data from Azure resources and applications into the workspace, enabling them to perform advanced analytics, query, and visualization tasks to gain insights into their operational performance and security posture. Azure Monitor also provides advanced alerting and notification capabilities to help organizations detect and respond to performance issues, security threats, and operational anomalies proactively. Administrators can configure alerts in Azure Monitor to monitor specific metrics, logs, or events from Azure resources and trigger automated response actions when predefined thresholds or conditions are met. To create an alert rule in Azure Monitor using the Azure portal, administrators can navigate to the Alerts section, click on the "New alert rule" button, and then follow the guided steps to define the alert criteria, conditions, and actions. Alternatively, you can create an alert rule using the Azure CLI by running the az monitor metrics alert create command, specifying parameters such as resource group, resource type, resource name, alert criteria, and actions. Once the alert rule is created, Azure Monitor monitors the specified metrics, logs, or events in real-time and triggers alerts when the defined thresholds or conditions are breached, enabling organizations to take timely corrective actions and prevent service disruptions or security incidents. Azure Monitor integrates with Azure Application Insights to provide organizations with comprehensive application performance monitoring (APM) capabilities, enabling them to monitor and analyze the performance, availability, and usage of their applications deployed in Azure and hybrid environments. Administrators can configure application insights in Azure Monitor to instrument *their applications with telemetry instrumentation code, such as SDKs or agents, to collect performance metrics, traces, exceptions, and dependencies from the application code and runtime environment. To configure application insights in Azure Monitor using the Azure portal, administrators can navigate to the Application Insights section, click on the "Create application insights" button, and then follow the guided steps to configure the application settings, such as name, region, application type, and instrumentation options. Alternatively, you can create an application insights resource using the Azure CLI by running the az monitor app-insights component create command, specifying parameters such as resource group, application name, region, and application type. Once the application insights resource is created, administrators can start instrumenting their applications with the provided instrumentation code, enabling them to collect and analyze performance telemetry data from the application code, infrastructure, and user interactions. Azure Monitor and Insights Tools provide organizations with powerful capabilities to monitor, analyze, and optimize the performance, availability, and security of their cloud workloads effectively. By leveraging the features and capabilities of Azure Monitor, organizations can gain deep insights into their Azure resources, applications, and infrastructure, enabling them to identify and resolve performance issues, security threats, and operational challenges proactively. Overall, Azure Monitor and Insights Tools are essential components of Microsoft Azure's ecosystem, empowering organizations to achieve operational excellence, agility, and resilience in the cloud.*

Optimizing costs and performance in Azure is paramount for organizations seeking to maximize the value of their cloud investments while ensuring efficient resource utilization and delivering high-quality services to their customers. Azure Cost Management and Billing is a comprehensive service provided by Microsoft Azure, designed to help organizations monitor, analyze, and optimize their cloud spending and usage. To access Azure Cost Management and Billing in the Azure portal, administrators can navigate to the Cost Management + Billing section, where they can view detailed reports and insights into their Azure spending, usage trends, and cost drivers. Alternatively, you can use the Azure CLI to access cost management data by running the az consumption usage list command, which retrieves usage data for a specified billing period and scope. By analyzing cost management data in Azure, organizations can identify opportunities to optimize their cloud spending, such as rightsizing underutilized resources, eliminating idle resources, and leveraging reserved instances or Azure Hybrid Benefit to reduce costs. Azure Cost Management and Billing also provide organizations with budgeting and forecasting capabilities, enabling them to set spending limits, monitor budget vs. actual spending, and receive alerts when spending exceeds predefined thresholds. Administrators can configure budgets in Azure Cost Management using the Azure portal by navigating to the Cost Management + Billing section, clicking on the "Budgets" tab, and then following the guided steps to create a new budget, specify the budget amount, duration, and alert conditions. Alternatively, you can create a budget using the Azure CLI by running the az consumption budget create command, specifying parameters such as budget name, amount, start and end dates, and alert threshold. By setting budgets in Azure Cost Management, organizations can proactively manage their cloud spending and prevent budget overruns, ensuring financial accountability and governance across their Azure environments. Azure Advisor is another valuable service provided by Microsoft Azure, offering personalized recommendations to help organizations optimize their Azure resources for cost, performance, security, and reliability. To access Azure Advisor recommendations in the Azure portal, administrators can navigate to the Advisor section, where they can view recommendations across various categories, such as cost optimization, performance, security, and operational excellence. Alternatively, you can use the Azure CLI to retrieve advisor recommendations by running the az advisor recommendation list command, which retrieves a list of recommendations for a specified subscription and resource group. By implementing Azure Advisor recommendations, organizations can improve the efficiency, reliability, and security of their Azure workloads while reducing costs and minimizing risks. Azure Reservations is a cost-saving offering provided by Microsoft Azure, enabling organizations to pre-purchase Azure resources, such as virtual machines, databases, and storage, at discounted rates for a one- or three-year term. To purchase reservations in Azure, administrators can navigate to the Reservations section of the Azure portal, where they can select the desired resource type, term length, and quantity, and then proceed to the checkout process to complete the reservation purchase. Alternatively, you can purchase reservations using the Azure CLI by running the az reservations catalog list-skus command to list available reservation SKUs, and then running the az reservations reservation create command to create a reservation for the desired resource type, term length, and quantity. By purchasing reservations in Azure, organizations can achieve significant cost savings compared to pay-as-you-go pricing, making it an effective cost optimization strategy for predictable and steady-state workloads. Azure Cost Management and Billing also offer cost allocation and chargeback capabilities, enabling organizations to track and allocate cloud costs to different departments, projects, or cost centers effectively. Administrators can configure cost allocation in Azure Cost Management using the Azure portal by navigating to the Cost Management + Billing section, clicking on the "Cost allocation" tab, and then following the guided steps to create allocation rules based on resource tags, resource groups, or other criteria. Alternatively, you can configure cost allocation using the Azure CLI by running the az consumption reservation summary command to retrieve reservation usage data, and then running the az consumption reservation detail command to retrieve reservation details and costs for a specified reservation. By implementing cost allocation in Azure Cost Management, organizations can achieve greater visibility, transparency, and accountability in their cloud spending, enabling them to make informed decisions and optimize resource utilization effectively. Overall, optimizing costs and performance in Azure is a continuous process that requires careful planning, monitoring, and management of cloud resources and spending. By leveraging the features and capabilities of Azure Cost Management and Billing, Azure Advisor, Azure

Reservations, and cost allocation, organizations can achieve significant cost savings, improve operational efficiency, and deliver better outcomes for their business and customers in the cloud.

Infrastructure as Code (IaC) with Azure Resource Manager (ARM) is a powerful approach to provisioning and managing Azure resources using declarative templates, enabling organizations to define and deploy their cloud infrastructure in a consistent, repeatable, and automated manner. Azure Resource Manager Templates, also known as ARM templates, are JSON files that describe the desired state of Azure resources and their relationships, configurations, and dependencies. To create an ARM template, developers can use any text editor or Integrated Development Environment (IDE) to write JSON code that specifies the resources, properties, and settings required for their Azure infrastructure. Alternatively, you can use tools like Visual Studio Code with Azure Resource Manager Tools extension to author and validate ARM templates efficiently. An example of an ARM template for deploying a virtual machine in Azure includes sections for defining the resources, such as the virtual machine, network interface, virtual network, and storage account, along with their configurations, such as size, location, and settings. By defining infrastructure as code with ARM templates, organizations can version-control their Azure infrastructure configurations, track changes over time, and collaborate effectively with team members using source control systems like Git. To deploy an ARM template to Azure using the Azure CLI, developers can use the az deployment group create command, specifying parameters such as resource group, deployment name, template file path, and template parameters file path. Alternatively, you can deploy an ARM template using the Azure portal by navigating to the desired resource group, clicking on the "Add" button, and then selecting "Template deployment" to upload and deploy the template file. Once the ARM template is deployed, Azure Resource Manager orchestrates the creation and configuration of the specified resources in the Azure environment, ensuring that the infrastructure is provisioned accurately and consistently according to the defined template. Azure Resource Manager also provides capabilities for managing and updating deployed resources using ARM templates, enabling organizations to automate the lifecycle management of their Azure infrastructure. By making changes to the ARM template and redeploying it to Azure, organizations can apply updates, modifications, or additions to their cloud resources in a controlled and predictable manner, ensuring that the infrastructure remains in sync with the desired configuration and state. Azure Resource Manager Templates support parameterization and template functions, enabling organizations to create reusable, parameterized templates that can be customized and adapted for different environments, scenarios, or use cases. By defining parameters in ARM templates, developers can make their templates more flexible and adaptable to various deployment scenarios, such as specifying resource names, sizes, locations, and configurations dynamically at deployment time. Template functions like concat, resourceId, uniqueString, and reference allow developers to dynamically generate values, resolve dependencies between resources, and retrieve information from existing resources, enabling them to build complex and scalable infrastructure solutions with ease. Azure Resource Manager also provides capabilities for managing resource dependencies, ordering, and parallel deployment, ensuring that resources are provisioned in the correct sequence and dependencies are resolved before proceeding with deployment. By specifying dependencies between resources in ARM templates, developers can define the relationships and dependencies between resources, ensuring that resources are created, updated, or deleted in the correct order to maintain consistency and integrity of the infrastructure. Azure Resource Manager Templates support conditionals and loops, enabling organizations to create dynamic, data-driven templates that adapt to different scenarios, conditions, or configurations. By using conditionals like if, equals, and not, developers can define logic and rules for deploying resources based on specific conditions or parameters, enabling them to create flexible and adaptable templates that handle different deployment scenarios gracefully. Loops like copy and for-each allow developers to iterate over collections or arrays of resources, properties, or configurations, enabling them to generate multiple instances of resources dynamically based on predefined patterns or templates. By leveraging the power of conditionals and loops in ARM templates, organizations can automate complex deployment scenarios, reduce manual intervention, and improve the efficiency and reliability of their infrastructure provisioning processes. Overall, Infrastructure as Code with Azure Resource Manager is a fundamental practice for organizations embracing cloud computing and DevOps principles, enabling them to automate and streamline the deployment, management, and governance of their Azure infrastructure at scale. By defining infrastructure configurations as code with ARM templates, organizations can achieve consistency, reliability, and agility in their cloud operations, empowering them to deliver value to their customers faster and more efficiently in the ever-evolving cloud *landscape.*

Azure DevOps Pipelines and Automation play a pivotal role in modern software development and deployment practices, enabling organizations to automate build, test, and deployment processes to deliver high-quality software applications efficiently and reliably. Azure DevOps, formerly known as Visual Studio Team Services (VSTS), provides a robust set of tools and services for DevOps practices, including version control, agile planning, continuous integration, continuous delivery, and release management. Azure Pipelines is a key component of Azure DevOps, offering cloud-hosted build and release services that allow organizations to automate the build and deployment of their applications across different platforms and environments. To create a pipeline in Azure DevOps, developers can navigate to the Pipelines section of the Azure DevOps portal and click on the "New pipeline" button to create a new pipeline using the visual designer or YAML configuration. Alternatively, you can use the Azure CLI to create a pipeline by running the az pipelines create command, specifying parameters such as project name, pipeline name, repository type, and configuration file path. Once the pipeline is created, developers can define stages, jobs, and tasks to automate the build, test, and deployment processes for their applications. Azure Pipelines supports integration with popular version control systems like Git and Subversion, enabling organizations to trigger pipeline runs automatically whenever code changes are committed or merged into the repository. By leveraging triggers in Azure Pipelines, organizations can implement continuous integration (CI) practices, ensuring that changes to the codebase are built, tested, and validated automatically to maintain code quality and integrity. Azure Pipelines also supports parallel and matrix builds, enabling organizations to accelerate build times and improve productivity by running multiple build jobs concurrently across different platforms, configurations, or environments. By configuring parallelism in Azure Pipelines, organizations can optimize resource utilization and reduce build wait times, enabling faster feedback loops and more efficient development workflows. Azure Pipelines offers a wide range of built-in and customizable tasks for building, testing, and deploying applications across various platforms and technologies, including .NET, Java, Node.js, Python, PHP, and containerized applications. Tasks like dotnet build, npm install, docker build, and kubectl apply allow developers to execute common build and deployment tasks seamlessly within the pipeline, ensuring consistency and reliability in the development and release processes. Azure Pipelines integrates with Azure Artifacts to enable organizations to store and manage artifacts, such as build outputs, binaries, and packages, securely and efficiently. By publishing artifacts in Azure Pipelines, organizations can share and distribute build artifacts across teams and environments, enabling seamless integration and deployment of applications across different stages of the release pipeline. Azure Pipelines supports flexible and customizable deployment strategies, including rolling deployments, canary releases, blue-green deployments, and manual approvals, enabling organizations to implement release automation practices that suit their specific requirements and business needs. By defining deployment strategies in Azure Pipelines, organizations can automate the deployment of applications to production environments reliably and safely, minimizing downtime and risk while maximizing availability and performance. Azure Pipelines provides comprehensive monitoring and analytics capabilities, enabling organizations to track pipeline execution, view build and release logs, and analyze performance metrics and trends effectively. By leveraging monitoring and analytics in Azure Pipelines, organizations can gain insights into their build and release processes, identify bottlenecks and inefficiencies, and continuously improve their DevOps practices to deliver better software faster and more reliably. Overall, Azure DevOps Pipelines and Automation are essential components of *modern software development and delivery pipelines, enabling organizations to automate and streamline their build, test, and deployment processes to accelerate time-to-market, improve quality, and enhance collaboration across development and operations teams. By adopting Azure Pipelines and Automation practices, organizations can achieve greater agility, reliability, and efficiency in delivering value to their customers and stakeholders in today's fast-paced and competitive digital landscape.*

Lift and Shift vs. Replatforming Strategies represent two distinct approaches to migrating applications and workloads to the cloud, each with its advantages, challenges, and considerations. Lift and Shift, also known as "rehosting," involves migrating applications from on-premises or legacy infrastructure to the cloud with minimal changes to the application code or architecture. The primary goal of Lift and Shift is to move applications quickly and efficiently to the cloud, leveraging cloud infrastructure and services to gain benefits such as scalability, availability, and cost-effectiveness without making significant modifications to the application. To perform a Lift and Shift migration, organizations can use tools like Azure Migrate, which automates the discovery, assessment, and migration of on-premises servers to Azure infrastructure. Using Azure Migrate, organizations can assess their on-premises environment, identify dependencies and performance characteristics, and estimate costs for running workloads in Azure. Once the assessment is complete, organizations can use

Azure Site Recovery to migrate virtual machines and physical servers to Azure with minimal downtime, ensuring a seamless transition to the cloud. Replatforming, on the other hand, involves making modifications to the application architecture or components to optimize them for cloud-native capabilities and services. Unlike Lift and Shift, which focuses on migration with minimal changes, Replatforming aims to modernize and optimize applications for the cloud, taking advantage of cloud-native features such as managed services, serverless computing, and microservices architectures. To execute a Replatforming strategy, organizations can leverage tools and services like Azure Kubernetes Service (AKS) to containerize applications and deploy them as microservices in a scalable and resilient manner. By containerizing applications, organizations can achieve greater agility, scalability, and efficiency in managing and deploying their applications in the cloud. Another approach to Replatforming is refactoring or "lift and reshape," which involves making changes to the application code or architecture to modernize it for cloud-native environments. For example, organizations can refactor monolithic applications into microservices architectures, adopt cloud-native databases and storage solutions, or *integrate with cloud-based AI and machine learning services to enhance application functionality and performance. By refactoring applications, organizations can unlock the full potential of cloud computing, enabling greater innovation, agility, and competitiveness in today's digital economy. When choosing between Lift and Shift and Replatforming strategies, organizations must consider factors such as application complexity, dependencies, regulatory compliance, and business requirements. Lift and Shift is ideal for simple, low-risk applications that require a quick and cost-effective migration to the cloud, while Replatforming is suitable for complex, mission-critical applications that require optimization and modernization for cloud-native environments. To evaluate which approach is best suited for their needs, organizations can perform a comprehensive assessment of their applications, infrastructure, and business objectives, taking into account factors such as performance, scalability, security, and cost. By carefully planning and executing their migration strategy, organizations can minimize risks, reduce downtime, and maximize the benefits of cloud computing, enabling them to innovate and grow with confidence in the cloud.*

Real-world Azure Migration Case Studies provide valuable insights into the challenges, strategies, and outcomes of organizations migrating their workloads to the Azure cloud platform. These case studies showcase diverse scenarios, industries, and migration approaches, offering practical examples and lessons learned for organizations embarking on their cloud migration journey. One such case study involves a global retail corporation that migrated its e-commerce platform to Azure to improve scalability, reliability, and performance. The company utilized Azure Site Recovery to migrate its virtual machines and databases to Azure Virtual Machines and Azure SQL Database, respectively, ensuring minimal downtime and data loss during the migration process. By leveraging Azure's global infrastructure and scalability, the company achieved significant improvements in website performance, response times, and user experience, resulting in increased customer satisfaction and sales revenue. Another compelling case study involves a healthcare organization that migrated its legacy on-premises infrastructure to Azure to modernize its IT systems and improve agility and compliance. The organization used Azure Migrate to assess its on-premises environment and identify migration dependencies, risks, and costs. Leveraging Azure Virtual

Machines, Azure Active Directory, and Azure Security Center, the organization migrated its applications, data, and identity services to Azure, ensuring compliance with industry regulations and standards. As a result, the organization achieved greater flexibility, scalability, and security in its IT operations, enabling it to deliver better patient care and support its growth initiatives effectively. Additionally, a financial services company successfully migrated its mission-critical trading platform to Azure to enhance performance, reliability, and compliance. The company employed Azure Data Factory, Azure SQL Database, and Azure Kubernetes Service to modernize its data processing and analytics capabilities, enabling real-time insights and decision-making for its traders and analysts. By migrating to Azure, the company reduced infrastructure costs, improved data security and compliance, and gained a competitive edge in the dynamic financial services industry. Furthermore, a manufacturing company migrated its on-premises SAP environment to Azure to streamline operations, reduce costs, and accelerate innovation. The company leveraged Azure Site Recovery, Azure Backup, and Azure Virtual Machines to migrate its SAP workloads and data to Azure, ensuring business continuity and data *protection throughout the migration process. With Azure, the company gained the flexibility to scale its SAP infrastructure on-demand, optimize costs, and integrate with other Azure services for advanced analytics, IoT, and AI capabilities. These real-world Azure migration case studies demonstrate the diverse benefits and opportunities of migrating to the cloud, from improving performance and scalability to enhancing security and compliance. By learning from these experiences and best practices, organizations can effectively plan, execute, and optimize their Azure migration initiatives, driving innovation, growth, and success in the cloud era.*

BOOK 3
VMWARE VIRTUALIZATION
OPTIMIZING CLOUD MIGRATION FOR ENTERPRISES

ROB BOTWRIGHT

The Evolution of Virtualization Technology has been a transformative journey, reshaping the landscape of IT infrastructure and enabling organizations to achieve greater flexibility, efficiency, and agility in managing their resources and workloads. Virtualization technology emerged in the late 20th century as a solution to the challenges of underutilized hardware resources and inefficient server provisioning processes. The introduction of hypervisor-based virtualization, pioneered by VMware in the early 2000s, revolutionized the way organizations deployed and managed their IT infrastructure. Hypervisor-based virtualization allows multiple virtual machines to run on a single physical server, enabling organizations to consolidate their workloads, improve resource utilization, and reduce hardware costs. To deploy virtual machines using VMware's hypervisor technology, organizations can use tools like VMware vSphere and vCenter Server to create, configure, and manage virtualized environments. With the rise of cloud computing in the 2010s, virtualization technology underwent further evolution, paving the way for the emergence of cloud-native virtualization platforms like Amazon Web Services (AWS), Microsoft Azure, and Google Cloud Platform (GCP). These cloud providers offer Infrastructure as a Service (IaaS) solutions that enable organizations to provision and manage virtual machines and other cloud resources on-demand, without the need for upfront hardware investments. To deploy virtual machines in the cloud using AWS, organizations can use the AWS Management Console or AWS Command Line Interface (CLI) to create instances, specify instance types, and configure networking and storage options. Similarly, in Microsoft Azure, organizations can use the Azure Portal or Azure CLI to deploy virtual machines, select virtual machine sizes, and customize virtual machine configurations to meet their specific requirements. As virtualization technology continued to evolve, containerization emerged as a complementary approach to virtualization, offering lightweight, portable, and scalable application deployment solutions. Containerization technology, popularized by Docker in the mid-2010s, enables organizations to package and deploy applications and their dependencies into isolated containers, ensuring consistency and reliability across different environments. To deploy containers using

Docker, organizations can use Docker CLI commands such as docker run, docker build, and docker-compose to create, manage, and orchestrate containers on Docker hosts or container orchestration platforms like Kubernetes. Kubernetes, an open-source container orchestration platform developed by Google, has become the de facto standard for managing containerized workloads at scale, providing features such as automated deployment, scaling, and management of containerized applications. To deploy applications on Kubernetes, organizations can use Kubernetes YAML manifest files or Kubernetes CLI commands such as kubectl apply to define and deploy application configurations, pods, services, and other Kubernetes resources. Looking ahead, the evolution of virtualization technology is expected to continue, driven by trends such as hybrid and multicloud adoption, edge computing, and serverless architectures. Organizations will increasingly leverage virtualization, containerization, and orchestration technologies to build and deploy modern, resilient, and scalable applications that meet the demands of today's digital economy. As virtualization technology evolves, organizations must stay abreast of emerging trends and best practices to harness the *full potential of these technologies and drive innovation and growth in the digital age. The Benefits and Use Cases of VMware Virtualization are multifaceted, offering organizations a wide array of advantages and opportunities to optimize their IT infrastructure, improve operational efficiency, and drive business innovation. VMware virtualization technology enables organizations to abstract computing resources from underlying hardware, creating virtual machines that run multiple operating systems and applications on a single physical server. One of the primary benefits of VMware virtualization is improved resource utilization, as organizations can consolidate their workloads onto fewer physical servers, reducing hardware costs and data center footprint. To deploy virtual machines using VMware virtualization technology, organizations can use the vSphere Client or vSphere Web Client to create, configure, and manage virtualized environments, specifying parameters such as CPU, memory, storage, and networking settings. Additionally, VMware virtualization enhances flexibility and agility, allowing organizations to dynamically allocate and reallocate computing resources based on changing workload demands, ensuring optimal performance and scalability. By virtualizing their IT infrastructure, organizations can quickly provision and deploy virtual machines, speeding up the application development and testing process and accelerating time-to-market for new products and services. Furthermore, VMware virtualization improves disaster recovery and business continuity capabilities, as organizations can replicate virtual machines and data to offsite locations, ensuring data protection and minimizing downtime in the event of hardware failures or disasters. To implement disaster recovery using VMware virtualization, organizations can use VMware Site Recovery Manager (SRM) to automate the failover and failback of virtual machines between primary and secondary data centers, ensuring seamless continuity of operations. Moreover, VMware virtualization enhances security and compliance by isolating workloads in separate virtual machines, preventing unauthorized access and minimizing the risk of data breaches and compliance violations. Organizations can implement security policies and controls at the virtual machine level, ensuring consistent enforcement and monitoring of security measures across their IT infrastructure. Additionally, VMware virtualization enables organizations to optimize their software licensing and maintenance costs by reducing the number of physical servers and operating system instances required to support their workloads. By consolidating their IT infrastructure onto a smaller number of physical servers, organizations can reduce software licensing fees and maintenance overhead, resulting in significant cost savings over time. Furthermore, VMware virtualization supports a wide range of use cases across industries, including server consolidation, desktop virtualization, development and testing, disaster recovery, and cloud migration. In the healthcare industry, for example, VMware virtualization enables hospitals and healthcare providers to consolidate electronic medical records (EMR) systems, medical imaging applications, and administrative workloads onto a centralized virtualized infrastructure, improving accessibility, scalability, and data security. Additionally, VMware virtualization supports desktop virtualization initiatives, allowing organizations to deliver virtual desktops and applications to end-users, enabling remote work, BYOD (Bring Your Own Device), and secure access to corporate resources from any location or device. Moreover, VMware virtualization facilitates cloud migration, enabling organizations to migrate their on-premises workloads to public or private cloud environments, leveraging VMware Cloud Foundation and VMware Cloud on AWS to seamlessly extend their VMware-based environments to the cloud. In summary, VMware virtualization offers a myriad of benefits and use cases for organizations seeking to modernize their IT infrastructure, improve agility, and drive innovation. By leveraging VMware virtualization technology, organizations can optimize resource utilization, enhance flexibility and agility, improve disaster recovery capabilities, enhance security and compliance, reduce costs, and support a wide range of use cases across industries, empowering them to achieve their business objectives and stay competitive in today's digital economy.*

The Overview of vSphere Architecture provides insight into the underlying components and mechanisms that make up VMware's virtualization platform, enabling organizations to understand the structure and functionality of vSphere environments. At the core of vSphere architecture is the hypervisor, which is responsible for abstracting physical hardware resources and creating virtual machines (VMs) that run multiple operating systems and applications. VMware's hypervisor, known as ESXi, is a lightweight, bare-metal hypervisor that installs directly on server hardware, allowing for efficient resource utilization and performance. To manage and administer vSphere environments, organizations can use the vSphere Client or vSphere Web Client, both of which provide graphical user interfaces (GUIs) for accessing and configuring vSphere resources. Additionally, VMware offers the vSphere Command-Line Interface (CLI), which allows administrators to perform advanced management tasks and automation using a command-line interface. Using the vSphere CLI, administrators can perform operations such as creating VMs, configuring networking, and monitoring performance. Within the vSphere architecture, key components include vCenter Server, which serves as a centralized management platform for vSphere environments, providing features such as VM provisioning, resource management, and performance monitoring. To deploy vCenter Server, organizations can use the vCenter Server Appliance (VCSA), which is a preconfigured virtual appliance that includes vCenter Server and its associated services. Alternatively, organizations can deploy vCenter Server on a Windows Server machine. vCenter Server interacts with ESXi hosts and manages their configuration, virtual machine lifecycle, and resource allocation. Another essential component of vSphere architecture is the Virtual Machine File System (VMFS), which is a high-performance file system designed for storing VM files such as virtual disks, configuration files, and snapshots. VMFS provides features such as thin provisioning, snapshots, and clustering, enabling organizations to efficiently manage and protect their VM data. To create and manage VMFS datastores, administrators can use the vSphere Client or vSphere Web Client to format storage devices and configure datastore properties. Additionally, vSphere architecture includes networking components such as vSphere Standard Switches (VSS) and vSphere Distributed Switches (VDS), which provide virtual networking capabilities *for connecting VMs to physical networks and each other. To configure networking in vSphere environments, administrators can use the vSphere Client or vSphere Web Client to create and manage virtual switches, port groups, and network policies. Moreover, vSphere architecture encompasses features such as vMotion, which enables live migration of VMs between ESXi hosts with zero downtime, and Distributed Resource Scheduler (DRS), which dynamically balances VM workloads across ESXi hosts to optimize performance and resource utilization. To leverage vMotion and DRS capabilities, organizations must ensure that their vSphere environment meets the necessary hardware and networking requirements and configure vMotion and DRS settings accordingly. Additionally, vSphere architecture includes features such as High Availability (HA) and Fault Tolerance (FT), which provide automated VM failover and continuous availability, respectively, in the event of host failures. To enable HA and FT in vSphere environments, administrators can configure HA and FT settings in vSphere Client or vSphere Web Client and monitor HA and FT status and events using vSphere tools and alerts. In summary, the Overview of vSphere Architecture provides organizations with a comprehensive understanding of the components, features, and capabilities of VMware's virtualization platform, empowering them to design, deploy, and* manage vSphere environments effectively. By leveraging vSphere architecture, organizations can optimize resource utilization, improve operational efficiency, and ensure the availability, scalability, and performance of their virtualized infrastructure. A Deep Dive into ESXi Hosts and vCenter Server unveils the intricate workings and critical roles these components play within VMware's vSphere environment, providing crucial insights into their functionalities, configurations, and management procedures. ESXi hosts serve as the foundational building blocks of a vSphere environment, acting as the hypervisor layer responsible for abstracting physical hardware resources and facilitating the creation and execution of virtual machines (VMs). The configuration and management of ESXi hosts are pivotal tasks for vSphere administrators, requiring meticulous attention to detail and adherence to best practices to ensure optimal performance and reliability. To deploy an ESXi host, administrators can utilize the VMware vSphere Installation Bundle (VIB) file, which contains the necessary software components for installing ESXi on bare-metal hardware. The installation process typically involves booting the host from the ESXi installation media and following the on-screen prompts to configure networking, storage, and other settings. Once deployed, ESXi hosts can be managed and monitored using the vSphere Client or *vSphere Web Client, which provide intuitive graphical interfaces for performing administrative tasks such as configuring host settings, monitoring resource utilization, and troubleshooting issues. Additionally, administrators can leverage the vSphere Command-Line Interface (CLI) to execute advanced management commands and automate tasks related to ESXi hosts, such as configuring networking settings or applying patches and updates. By accessing the ESXi Shell or using SSH to connect to the host's command line interface, administrators can run commands such as esxcli to perform various management tasks, including viewing system information, managing virtual machines, and troubleshooting network connectivity issues. Furthermore, ESXi hosts can be configured to participate in vSphere clusters, which enable advanced features such as vMotion, Distributed Resource Scheduler (DRS), and High Availability (HA). vMotion allows administrators to migrate running VMs between ESXi hosts with zero downtime, facilitating workload balancing and hardware maintenance tasks. To initiate a vMotion migration, administrators can use the vSphere Client or vSphere Web Client to select the VM to be migrated and specify the destination ESXi host. Similarly, DRS automatically balances VM workloads across ESXi hosts within a cluster based on resource utilization and configured policies, ensuring optimal* performance and resource utilization. Administrators can configure DRS settings, such as automation levels and migration thresholds, using the vSphere Client or vSphere Web Client to customize DRS behavior to suit their organization's needs. Moreover, HA provides automated VM failover in the event of host failures, ensuring continuous availability and minimizing downtime for critical workloads. To configure HA settings, administrators can use the vSphere Client or vSphere Web Client to enable and configure HA clusters, specify admission control policies, and define VM restart priorities. On the other hand, vCenter Server serves as the centralized management platform for vSphere environments, providing a unified interface for managing ESXi hosts, VMs, storage, networking, and other vSphere components. To deploy vCenter Server, organizations can choose between the vCenter Server Appliance (VCSA) or a Windows-based installation, each offering its advantages and considerations. The VCSA is a preconfigured virtual appliance that includes vCenter Server and its associated services, simplifying deployment and management tasks. To deploy the VCSA, administrators can use the vSphere Client or vSphere Web Client to import the appliance OVA file, configure networking and storage settings, and specify deployment options such as deployment size and data retention policies. Alternatively, *organizations can deploy vCenter Server on a Windows Server machine, following the installation wizard prompts to configure database settings, authentication options, and other parameters. Once deployed, vCenter Server provides a range of management capabilities, including VM provisioning, performance monitoring, and automation through features such as vSphere Update Manager (VUM) and vSphere Distributed Switch (VDS). VUM allows administrators to automate patch management and update ESXi hosts and VMs to ensure security and compliance with vendor recommendations. To use VUM, administrators can navigate to the Update Manager tab in the vSphere Client or vSphere Web Client and follow the guided workflows to create baselines, scan hosts for compliance, and remediate any issues found. Additionally, VDS extends the functionality of vSphere Standard Switches (VSS) by providing centralized management and advanced networking features such as Network I/O Control (NIOC) and traffic shaping. Administrators can use the vSphere Client or vSphere Web Client to create and manage VDS instances, configure network policies, and monitor network traffic and performance. In summary, a deep dive into ESXi hosts and vCenter Server reveals the critical roles these components play within vSphere environments, offering organizations the tools and capabilities needed to* deploy, manage, and optimize their virtualized infrastructure effectively. Through meticulous configuration, monitoring, and administration, organizations can harness the full potential of ESXi hosts and vCenter Server to achieve greater flexibility, scalability, and reliability in their IT operations.

Creating and Configuring Virtual Machines is a fundamental aspect of managing virtualized infrastructure in environments like VMware's vSphere, Microsoft's Azure, or Amazon Web Services (AWS), and it involves several essential steps to provision and customize VMs to meet specific workload requirements. In VMware vSphere, one of the most widely used virtualization platforms, creating a virtual machine typically begins with accessing the vSphere Client or vSphere Web Client, where administrators can initiate the VM creation process by navigating to the appropriate menu option, which may vary depending on the version of vSphere being used. Once in the VM creation wizard, administrators can specify various parameters for the new VM, such as its name, guest operating system, and hardware configuration, including CPU, memory, disk, and network settings, to ensure that it meets the workload's resource requirements. For example, to create a new VM named "VM1" with 4 vCPUs, 8GB of memory, and a 100GB virtual disk in VMware vSphere using the command line interface, administrators can use the esxcli command followed by parameters to define the VM's configuration, including CPU, memory, and storage specifications. After specifying the VM's hardware configuration, administrators can proceed to customize additional settings, such as enabling VMware Tools for enhanced VM management and performance, configuring virtual machine options like power management and time synchronization, and attaching ISO images or virtual hardware devices for OS installation or additional functionality. Once all configuration settings are finalized, administrators can review the VM's summary and confirm the creation process to deploy the new virtual machine on the selected ESXi host or cluster within the vSphere environment. Similarly, in cloud platforms like Microsoft Azure and AWS, creating and configuring virtual machines follows a similar process but with platform-specific tools and interfaces. In Microsoft Azure, administrators can create virtual machines using the Azure Portal, Azure CLI, or Azure PowerShell by selecting the appropriate options to define the VM's specifications, such as its size, operating system, networking configuration, and storage requirements. For instance, to create a new VM named "VM1" with 4 vCPUs, 8GB of memory, and a 100GB OS disk in Microsoft Azure using Azure CLI, administrators can use the *az vm create* command followed by parameters to specify the VM's configuration details. Similarly, in AWS, administrators can use the AWS Management Console, AWS CLI, or AWS SDKs to create virtual machines, known as Amazon EC2 instances, by selecting the desired instance type, AMI (Amazon Machine Image), and configuration options, such as instance size, storage type, and networking settings. For example, to launch a new EC2 instance named "VM1" with 4 vCPUs, 8GB of memory, and a 100GB EBS (Elastic Block Store) volume in AWS using the AWS CLI, administrators can use the *aws ec2 run-instances* command followed by parameters to specify the instance's configuration. Once the virtual machine is created and deployed, administrators can connect to it remotely using protocols like SSH (Secure Shell) for Linux-based VMs or RDP (Remote Desktop Protocol) for Windows-based VMs to perform initial configuration tasks, such as installing software, configuring network settings, and securing the operating system. Additionally, administrators can further customize the VM's configuration post-deployment by attaching additional storage volumes, configuring security *groups and firewalls to control inbound and outbound traffic, and installing agent-based tools for monitoring, management, and security purposes. Overall, creating and configuring virtual machines is a foundational task in managing virtualized infrastructure, whether in on-premises data centers or cloud environments, and requires careful consideration of hardware specifications, operating system requirements, and workload demands to ensure optimal performance, scalability, and reliability. Virtual Machine Templates and Cloning Techniques are indispensable tools in virtualized environments, providing administrators with efficient methods for deploying standardized VM configurations and rapidly provisioning new virtual machines. A virtual machine template serves as a master image from which identical copies, or clones, can be created, streamlining the process of VM deployment and ensuring consistency across the virtual infrastructure. In VMware vSphere, administrators can create virtual machine templates by first configuring a VM with the desired operating system, software, and configurations, then converting it into a template using the vSphere Client or vSphere Web Client. To create a template from an existing VM in vSphere, administrators can power off the VM,* right-click on it, and select the "Convert to Template" option. Alternatively, administrators can use the vmware-cmd command in the ESXi Shell or SSH to convert a VM to a template. Once converted, the template serves as a blueprint for deploying new VMs with identical configurations, saving time and ensuring consistency. To deploy a new VM from a template in vSphere, administrators can use the "Deploy from Template" option in the vSphere Client or vSphere Web Client, where they can specify parameters such as the VM name, location, and customization settings. Similarly, in Microsoft Azure, administrators can leverage Azure Managed Images or Azure Resource Manager (ARM) templates to create reusable templates for VM deployment. Managed Images allow administrators to capture a generalized VM as a reusable image, which can then be used to provision new VMs with the same configuration. To create a managed image in Azure, administrators can use the Azure Portal, Azure CLI, or Azure PowerShell to generalize a VM and create an image from it using commands such as az vm generalize and az image create. Once the image is created, administrators can use it to deploy new VMs using the Azure Portal, Azure CLI, or Azure PowerShell by specifying the image name and *other configuration settings. ARM templates, on the other hand, enable administrators to define infrastructure as code using JSON (JavaScript Object Notation) templates, which can be version-controlled and deployed programmatically to provision entire environments, including VMs, networking, and storage resources. To deploy a VM from an ARM template, administrators can use the Azure Portal, Azure CLI, or Azure PowerShell to specify the template file and parameter values, which define the VM's configuration and properties. In Amazon Web Services (AWS), administrators can use Amazon Machine Images (AMIs) to create reusable templates for EC2 instance deployment. An AMI contains the necessary operating system, software, and configuration settings required to launch an EC2 instance with specific characteristics. To create an AMI in AWS, administrators can use the AWS Management Console, AWS CLI, or AWS SDKs to create an Image from an existing EC2 instance or from an Amazon EBS (Elastic Block Store) volume snapshot. Once the AMI is created, administrators can use it to launch new EC2 instances using the AWS Management Console, AWS CLI, or AWS SDKs by specifying the AMI ID and other instance parameters. Additionally, administrators can use*

EC2 Auto Scaling groups to automatically launch and manage a fleet of EC2 instances based on predefined scaling policies, ensuring high availability and scalability for applications and services. Overall, Virtual Machine Templates and Cloning Techniques play a crucial role in simplifying and automating VM deployment processes, enabling administrators to efficiently provision, manage, and scale virtualized infrastructure in on-premises data centers and cloud environments.

Storage Types and Protocols in VMware encompass a diverse range of options for storing virtual machine data, each tailored to specific performance, scalability, and cost requirements. VMware supports various storage types, including direct-attached storage (DAS), network-attached storage (NAS), and storage area networks (SANs), providing flexibility in designing storage solutions for virtualized environments. DAS refers to storage devices directly connected to a host server, such as internal hard drives or external storage arrays, offering simplicity and low latency but limited scalability and redundancy. VMware supports DAS through technologies like VMware Virtual Volumes (VVols), which enable granular storage management and integration with virtual machines. To configure DAS in VMware, administrators can use the vSphere Client or vSphere Web Client to add local storage devices to ESXi hosts and create datastores for VM storage. NAS provides shared storage over a network, allowing multiple hosts to access files and data concurrently, making it suitable for environments requiring shared access and file-level storage protocols like NFS (Network File System) or

SMB (Server Message Block). VMware integrates seamlessly with NAS solutions, enabling administrators to use NFS datastores for VM storage and leveraging features like Storage vMotion for live VM migration between datastores. To configure NAS storage in VMware, administrators can mount NFS shares to ESXi hosts using the vSphere Client or vSphere Web Client and create NFS datastores for VM storage. SANs deliver block-level storage over a high-speed network, offering performance, scalability, and advanced features like snapshots, replication, and thin provisioning, making them ideal for mission-critical applications and high-performance workloads. VMware supports SANs through protocols like Fibre Channel (FC), iSCSI (Internet Small Computer System Interface), and Fibre Channel over Ethernet (FCoE), allowing administrators to leverage features like VMware vSphere Storage APIs for Array Integration (VAAI) for enhanced storage operations. To configure SAN storage in VMware, administrators can use the vSphere Client or vSphere Web Client to create iSCSI or Fibre Channel storage adapters on ESXi hosts and connect them to SAN arrays, then create VMFS (Virtual Machine File System) datastores for VM storage. Additionally, VMware offers software-defined storage solutions like VMware vSAN (Virtual SAN), which aggregates local storage devices from multiple ESXi hosts into a shared datastore, providing scalable, high-performance storage with integrated data services like deduplication, compression, and erasure coding. To deploy vSAN in VMware, administrators can use the vSphere Client or vSphere Web Client to enable vSAN on ESXi hosts and configure storage policies to define performance and availability requirements for VMs. VMware also supports external storage arrays from leading vendors, allowing administrators to integrate third-party SAN and NAS solutions with vSphere environments seamlessly. By leveraging VMware Storage APIs and features like Storage DRS (Distributed Resource Scheduler) and Storage I/O Control (SIOC), administrators can optimize storage performance, utilization, and reliability in VMware environments, ensuring that virtualized workloads operate efficiently and reliably. Overall, Storage Types and Protocols in VMware provide administrators with a comprehensive array of options for designing and implementing storage solutions that meet the unique needs of their virtualized infrastructure, enabling them to achieve optimal performance, scalability, and data protection. Storage Policies and Datastores Management are crucial aspects of storage administration in virtualized environments, encompassing the creation, configuration, and optimization of datastores and storage policies to meet the performance, availability, and compliance requirements of virtual machines. Datastores serve as repositories for virtual machine files, including virtual disks, templates, and ISO images, providing the storage capacity and performance necessary for running workloads efficiently. In VMware vSphere, administrators can manage datastores using the vSphere Client or vSphere Web Client, where they can create, delete, and resize datastores as well as monitor datastore usage and performance metrics. To create a datastore in VMware vSphere, administrators can navigate to the Storage section of the vSphere Client or vSphere Web Client, select the storage device or storage pool they want to use, and follow the prompts to create a new datastore with the desired configuration settings. Datastores can be provisioned from various storage types, including local storage, NFS shares, SAN LUNs, and VMware vSAN, allowing administrators to tailor storage solutions to the specific needs of their virtualized environment. Once created, datastores can be managed and monitored to ensure optimal performance and availability for virtual machine workloads. Storage policies, also known as storage profiles, define the characteristics and capabilities of storage resources, such as performance tiers, redundancy levels, and data services, enabling administrators to apply consistent storage management policies across multiple datastores and virtual machines. In VMware vSphere, administrators can create and manage storage policies using the vSphere Client or vSphere Web Client, where they can define policy rules based on storage capabilities and requirements, such as RAID levels, replication settings, and snapshot schedules. To create a storage policy in VMware vSphere, administrators can navigate to the Policies and Profiles section of the vSphere Client or vSphere Web Client, select Storage Policies, and follow the prompts to create a new policy with the desired settings. Once created, storage policies can be assigned to individual virtual machines or virtual machine templates, ensuring that VMs are provisioned with the appropriate storage attributes based on their performance and availability needs. Storage policies can also be used in conjunction with features like VMware Storage DRS (Distributed Resource Scheduler) and VMware Storage I/O Control (SIOC) to automate storage provisioning and optimization based on workload demands. Additionally, administrators can use storage policies to enforce data compliance requirements, such as data encryption, data retention, and data locality, ensuring that sensitive data is stored and managed according to organizational policies and regulatory standards. Overall, Storage Policies and Datastores Management are essential components of storage administration in virtualized environments, enabling *administrators to provision, manage, and optimize storage resources to support the performance, availability, and compliance needs of virtual machine workloads effectively.*

VMware vSphere Networking Basics encompasses
the fundamental concepts, components, and
configurations of networking in vSphere
environments, providing the foundation for
building and managing network infrastructures to
support virtualized workloads effectively.
Networking in VMware vSphere revolves around
virtual switches, port groups, and network
adapters, which collectively enable
communication between virtual machines, ESXi
hosts, and external networks. Virtual switches,
such as the vSphere Standard Switch (vSS) and the
vSphere Distributed Switch (vDS), act as software-
based network switches within ESXi hosts,
facilitating traffic routing between virtual
machines and uplink connections to physical
networks. In VMware vSphere, administrators can
create and manage virtual switches using the
vSphere Client or vSphere Web Client, where they
can configure switch settings, add or remove port
groups, and configure uplink adapters for network
connectivity. To create a virtual switch in VMware
vSphere using the command line interface (CLI),

administrators can use the esxcli network vswitch standard add command, specifying parameters such as the switch name, number of ports, and VLAN settings. Once created, virtual switches can be configured with port groups, which define network connectivity and settings for virtual machine interfaces, such as VLAN tagging, traffic shaping, and security policies. In VMware vSphere, administrators can create port groups using the vSphere Client or vSphere Web Client, where they can specify port group settings and associate them with virtual switches. To create a port group in VMware vSphere using the CLI, administrators can use the esxcli network vswitch standard portgroup add command, providing parameters such as the port group name, VLAN ID, and VLAN trunking settings. Additionally, administrators can configure network adapters for ESXi hosts to enable communication with virtual machines and external networks. Network adapters in VMware vSphere can be physical NICs (Network Interface Cards) or virtual NICs (vmNICs) that provide connectivity to virtual machines. In VMware vSphere, administrators can configure network adapters using the vSphere Client or vSphere Web Client, where they can specify adapter settings, such as speed, duplex mode, and VLAN tagging. To configure a network adapter in VMware vSphere using the CLI, administrators can use the esxcli network nic set command, specifying parameters such as the adapter name and desired settings. VMware vSphere also supports advanced networking features, such as VLANs (Virtual LANs), NIC teaming, and network I/O control (NIOC), which enable administrators to segment traffic, improve network redundancy, and prioritize network resources for virtualized workloads. VLANs allow administrators to logically partition network traffic into separate broadcast domains, providing isolation and security for different types of traffic. In VMware vSphere, administrators can configure VLANs using the vSphere Client or vSphere Web Client, where they can assign VLAN IDs to port groups and virtual switches. To configure VLANs in VMware vSphere using the CLI, administrators can use the esxcli network vswitch standard portgroup set command, specifying parameters such as the port group name and VLAN ID. NIC teaming enables administrators to aggregate multiple network adapters into a single logical interface, increasing network throughput and fault tolerance. In VMware vSphere, administrators can configure NIC teaming using the vSphere Client or vSphere Web Client, where they can specify teaming policies and load balancing algorithms. To configure NIC teaming in

VMware vSphere using the CLI, administrators can use the esxcli network vswitch standard policy failover set command, specifying parameters such as the vSwitch name and failover settings. Network I/O control (NIOC) allows administrators to prioritize and allocate network bandwidth to different types of traffic, such as management, vMotion, and virtual machine traffic, ensuring that critical workloads receive adequate network resources. In VMware vSphere, administrators can configure NIOC using the vSphere Client or vSphere Web Client, where they can create network resource pools and assign them to port groups. To configure NIOC in VMware vSphere using the CLI, administrators can use the esxcli network vswitch dvs qos vmware command, specifying parameters such as the distributed switch name and resource allocation settings. Overall, VMware vSphere Networking Basics provides administrators with the knowledge and tools necessary to design, configure, and manage network infrastructures in virtualized environments effectively, ensuring reliable and efficient communication between virtual machines and external networks. Configuring Virtual Switches and Port Groups is a crucial aspect of networking in virtualized environments, enabling administrators to manage network connectivity and traffic flow within VMware vSphere infrastructures effectively. Virtual switches, such as the vSphere Standard Switch (vSS) and the vSphere Distributed Switch (vDS), serve as software-based networking components that connect virtual machines to each other and to external networks. In VMware vSphere, administrators can create and configure virtual switches using the vSphere Client or vSphere Web Client, where they can define switch settings, add or remove port groups, and configure uplink adapters for network connectivity. To create a virtual switch in VMware vSphere, administrators can use the esxcli network vswitch standard add command, specifying parameters such as the switch name, number of ports, and VLAN settings. Once created, virtual switches can be configured with port groups, which define network connectivity and settings for virtual machine interfaces. Port groups allow administrators to segment network traffic, apply traffic shaping and security policies, and control access to network resources. In VMware vSphere, administrators can create port groups using the vSphere Client or vSphere Web Client, where they can specify port group settings and associate them with virtual switches. To create a port group in VMware vSphere using the CLI, administrators can *use the esxcli network vswitch standard portgroup add command, providing parameters such as the port group name, VLAN ID, and VLAN trunking settings. Additionally, administrators can configure uplink adapters for virtual switches to enable connectivity to external networks. Uplink adapters provide network connectivity for virtual machines and ESXi hosts, allowing them to communicate with other devices on the network. In VMware vSphere, administrators can configure uplink adapters using the vSphere Client or vSphere Web Client, where they can specify adapter settings such as speed, duplex mode, and VLAN tagging. To configure an uplink adapter in VMware vSphere using the CLI, administrators can use the esxcli network nic set command, specifying parameters such as the adapter name and desired settings. Furthermore, administrators can configure advanced networking features such as VLANs (Virtual LANs), NIC teaming, and network I/O control (NIOC) to optimize network performance and reliability. VLANs allow administrators to logically segment network traffic into separate broadcast domains, providing isolation and security for different types of traffic. In VMware vSphere, administrators can configure VLANs using the vSphere Client or vSphere Web Client, where they can assign VLAN IDs to port* groups and virtual switches. To configure VLANs in VMware vSphere using the CLI, administrators can use the esxcli network vswitch standard portgroup set command, specifying parameters such as the port group name and VLAN ID. NIC teaming enables administrators to aggregate multiple network adapters into a single logical interface, increasing network throughput and fault tolerance. In VMware vSphere, administrators can configure NIC teaming using the vSphere Client or vSphere Web Client, where they can specify teaming policies and load balancing algorithms. To configure NIC teaming in VMware vSphere using the CLI, administrators can use the esxcli network vswitch standard policy failover set command, specifying parameters such as the vSwitch name and failover settings. Network I/O control (NIOC) allows administrators to prioritize and allocate network bandwidth to different types of traffic, ensuring that critical workloads receive adequate network resources. In VMware vSphere, administrators can configure NIOC using the vSphere Client or vSphere Web Client, where they can create network resource pools and assign them to port groups. To configure NIOC in VMware vSphere using the CLI, administrators can use the esxcli network vswitch dvs qos vmware command, specifying parameters such as the *distributed switch name and resource allocation settings. Overall, Configuring Virtual Switches and Port Groups is essential for building and managing network infrastructures in VMware vSphere environments, providing administrators with the flexibility and control to optimize network performance, reliability, and security for virtualized workloads.*

Securing ESXi Hosts and vCenter Server is paramount in maintaining the integrity and confidentiality of virtualized environments, safeguarding against potential security threats and unauthorized access. One crucial aspect of securing ESXi hosts is ensuring that only authorized personnel can access and manage the hypervisor. To achieve this, administrators can configure strong authentication mechanisms such as Secure Shell (SSH) and lockdown mode. SSH allows administrators to securely access ESXi hosts remotely using encrypted connections, while lockdown mode restricts direct host access to the vSphere Web Client or vSphere Client, preventing unauthorized SSH or Direct Console User Interface (DCUI) access. To enable SSH on an ESXi host, administrators can use the esxcli system ssh set command, specifying parameters such as the SSH service start or stop. Additionally, administrators can configure lockdown mode using the vSphere Web Client, navigating to the host's configuration tab and enabling the lockdown mode option. Another critical aspect of securing ESXi hosts is applying security patches and updates regularly to mitigate vulnerabilities and ensure compliance with security standards. Administrators can leverage VMware Update Manager (VUM) to automate the patching process, scanning ESXi hosts for missing patches and applying updates accordingly. To scan and remediate ESXi hosts using VUM, administrators can use the vSphere Web Client, navigating to the Update Manager tab and creating a new baseline group containing the desired patches. They can then attach the baseline group to the ESXi hosts and initiate a scan and remediation process. Furthermore, administrators can enhance ESXi host security by configuring firewall settings to control inbound and outbound network traffic. ESXi hosts include a built-in firewall that allows administrators to create firewall rules to permit or deny specific types of traffic based on port numbers and protocols. To configure firewall rules on an ESXi host, administrators can use the esxcli network firewall ruleset set command, specifying parameters such as the firewall ruleset name and action. Moreover, administrators can strengthen ESXi host security by implementing role-based access control (RBAC) to manage user privileges and permissions effectively. RBAC allows administrators to assign roles to users or groups, granting them specific privileges based on their responsibilities and requirements. In VMware vSphere, administrators can create custom roles using the vSphere Web Client, defining role privileges such as virtual machine management, host configuration, or network administration. To create a custom role in VMware vSphere, administrators can navigate to the Roles tab in the vSphere Web Client's administration section and click the "Add Role" button, specifying the role name and privileges. In addition to securing ESXi hosts, it is equally essential to secure the vCenter Server, which serves as the central management platform for VMware vSphere environments. Securing the vCenter Server involves implementing measures such as enabling strong authentication, configuring access controls, and encrypting sensitive data. Administrators can enhance vCenter Server security by integrating it with external identity providers such as Active Directory (AD) or Lightweight Directory Access Protocol (LDAP), allowing users to authenticate using their existing credentials. To configure identity sources in vCenter Server, administrators can use the vSphere Web Client, navigating to the Single Sign-On (SSO) configuration tab and adding the desired identity provider. Additionally, administrators can implement access controls in vCenter Server by defining permission policies to control user access to inventory objects and management tasks. Permission policies allow administrators to assign privileges to users or groups based on their roles and responsibilities, limiting access to sensitive operations such as VM creation, deletion, or configuration changes. To configure permissions in vCenter Server, administrators can use the vSphere Web Client, navigating to the Permissions tab and assigning roles to users or groups. Furthermore, administrators can enhance vCenter Server security by encrypting sensitive data such as passwords, certificates, and configuration files. VMware vSphere supports encryption for various components, including vCenter Server, ESXi hosts, and virtual machines, using technologies such as VMware vSphere VM Encryption (VMVE) and VMware vSAN Encryption. To enable encryption for vCenter Server, administrators can use the vSphere Web Client, navigating to the vCenter Server settings and enabling the encryption option. Overall, Securing ESXi Hosts and vCenter Server is critical for protecting VMware vSphere environments from security threats and ensuring compliance with industry regulations and best practices. By implementing robust security measures such as strong authentication, patch management, firewall configuration, RBAC, and *data encryption, administrators can mitigate risks and maintain the confidentiality, integrity, and availability of their virtualized infrastructure.*

Implementing Role-Based Access Control (RBAC) is essential for organizations to effectively manage user permissions and access rights within their IT infrastructure, ensuring that users have appropriate access to resources based on their roles and responsibilities. RBAC provides a granular level of control over who can perform specific actions on resources, reducing the risk of unauthorized access and potential security breaches. One of the key components of RBAC is defining roles that encompass a set of permissions or privileges required to perform certain tasks. These roles are then assigned to users or groups within the organization, dictating their level of access to resources. In many systems, including cloud platforms and operating systems, RBAC is implemented using a combination of predefined roles and custom roles tailored to the organization's specific needs. For example, in the context of cloud platforms such as AWS, Azure, or Google Cloud Platform (GCP), RBAC is typically managed through a centralized identity and access management (IAM) service. In AWS, IAM allows administrators to create IAM policies that define permissions for various actions on AWS resources. These policies can be attached to IAM roles, which are then assigned to IAM users or groups. To create a custom IAM policy in AWS, administrators can use the AWS Management Console or the AWS Command Line Interface (CLI), specifying the desired permissions in JSON format and attaching the policy to an IAM role using the aws iam put-role-policy command. Similarly, in Azure, RBAC is managed through Azure Active Directory (AD), where administrators can create custom roles with specific permissions using Azure PowerShell or the Azure CLI. These custom roles can then be assigned to users or groups within the Azure AD directory. To create a custom role in Azure using the Azure CLI, administrators can use the az role definition create command, specifying parameters such as the role name, description, and permissions. Once roles are defined and assigned, administrators must carefully manage and monitor user access to ensure that permissions are aligned with organizational policies and regulatory requirements. This includes regularly reviewing and auditing role assignments to identify and remediate any potential security risks or compliance issues. In addition to managing access at the role level, RBAC often involves the use of resource groups or *organizational units to logically group related resources and apply access controls more efficiently. Resource groups allow administrators to define access policies that apply to all resources within the group, simplifying management and ensuring consistency across the environment. For example, in AWS, administrators can use AWS Organizations to centrally manage access policies and permissions across multiple AWS accounts and resources. This involves creating organizational units (OUs) and applying policies that govern access to resources within each OU. To create an OU in AWS Organizations, administrators can use the AWS Management Console or the AWS CLI, using the create-organizational-unit command. Overall, implementing RBAC is a fundamental aspect of IT security and governance, enabling organizations to enforce least privilege principles and mitigate the risk of unauthorized access. By defining granular roles and permissions, assigning them to users or groups, and regularly reviewing access controls, organizations can maintain a secure and compliant environment while empowering users to perform their roles effectively.*

VMware High Availability (HA) Configuration is a critical aspect of ensuring the resilience and availability of virtualized environments. HA is a feature provided by VMware vSphere that enables automatic restart of virtual machines (VMs) on alternative host servers in the event of a host failure. This capability helps minimize downtime and maintain service continuity by quickly recovering from hardware failures. Configuring VMware HA involves several steps to enable and customize the feature according to the organization's requirements. In VMware vSphere, HA is typically configured at the cluster level, where multiple ESXi hosts are grouped together to form a cluster. To configure HA, administrators can use the vSphere Web Client or the vSphere Client interface, accessing the cluster settings and navigating to the "Configure" tab. From there, they can select "vSphere Availability" and click on "Edit" to enable HA and adjust settings such as admission control policies and VM monitoring options. Admission control policies determine how resources are reserved to ensure sufficient capacity for VM restarts in case of host failures. There are several admission control policies available, including "Host Failures Cluster Tolerates" and "Percentage of Cluster Resources Reserved." These policies help prevent resource contention and ensure that VMs can be restarted successfully on remaining hosts within the cluster. Additionally, administrators can configure VM monitoring settings to determine how HA monitors the status of VMs and triggers failover actions. This includes options such as "VM and Application Monitoring" and "VM Monitoring Only," which use heartbeat mechanisms to detect VM and application failures. Once HA is enabled and configured, VMware vSphere continuously monitors the health of ESXi hosts and VMs within the cluster. In the event of a host failure, HA automatically detects the failure and triggers a failover process to restart affected VMs on other hosts in the cluster. This process involves several steps, including VM shutdown on the failed host, VM restart on a healthy host, and reestablishment of network connectivity and storage access. During failover, HA ensures that VMs are restarted in a prioritized manner based on predefined rules and dependencies. For example, VMs with higher priority or critical applications may be restarted first to minimize service disruption. Administrators can monitor HA events and failover actions using vSphere tools such as the vSphere Web Client, which provides visibility into cluster status, VM availability, and failover events. In addition to basic HA configuration, VMware offers advanced features and capabilities to enhance availability and resilience in virtualized environments. This includes features such as vSphere Fault Tolerance (FT), which provides continuous availability for VMs by maintaining a secondary VM instance that mirrors the primary VM in real-time. FT ensures zero downtime and zero data loss for critical applications by automatically switching to the secondary VM in the event of a primary VM failure. To configure FT, administrators can enable the feature at the VM level and specify the number of secondary instances to maintain. VMware HA Configuration is a fundamental aspect of vSphere architecture, providing essential capabilities for ensuring high availability and resilience in virtualized environments. By following best practices and properly configuring HA settings, organizations can minimize downtime, improve service reliability, and enhance overall business continuity.

VMware vSphere Replication and Site Recovery Manager (SRM) are integral components of disaster recovery (DR) and business continuity *strategies, offering robust solutions for replicating and recovering virtualized workloads in case of unplanned outages or disasters. vSphere Replication provides asynchronous replication of VMs at the virtual machine disk (VMDK) level, allowing organizations to create replica copies of VMs to a secondary site or storage location. This replication occurs over the network, asynchronously, with configurable recovery point objectives (RPOs) to meet the organization's data protection requirements. Configuring vSphere Replication involves several steps, beginning with the installation of the vSphere Replication appliance, which serves as the replication engine. Once deployed, administrators can configure replication settings for individual VMs through the vSphere Web Client or the vSphere Client interface. This includes selecting the replication target, defining replication schedules, and specifying retention policies for replicated data. To enable replication for a VM, administrators can navigate to the VM's settings, select the "Manage" tab, and choose "Configure Replication." From there, they can specify the replication target, such as a vCenter Server or a vSphere Replication server, and configure replication settings according to the organization's DR requirements. Additionally, administrators can* monitor replication status and performance using vSphere Replication's built-in monitoring and reporting tools, which provide visibility into replication jobs, data transfer rates, and replication lag. Site Recovery Manager (SRM) extends the capabilities of vSphere Replication by providing automated orchestration and failover procedures for disaster recovery scenarios. SRM simplifies the process of DR planning, testing, and execution, allowing organizations to streamline their recovery operations and minimize downtime during outages. Configuring SRM involves deploying the SRM appliance and pairing it with vCenter Server instances at both the protected and recovery sites. Once paired, administrators can create recovery plans that define the sequence of steps to execute during a failover event, including VM power-on, network reconfiguration, and application startup procedures. To create a recovery plan in SRM, administrators can use the SRM interface to specify the VMs to protect, recovery site resources, and recovery priorities. They can also define recovery groups to group related VMs and specify dependencies between VMs to ensure proper recovery order. Once the recovery plan is created, administrators can test failover procedures in a non-disruptive manner using SRM's built-in testing capabilities. This *allows organizations to validate their DR plans and ensure readiness for real-world failover scenarios. In the event of a disaster or outage, SRM automates the failover process, orchestrating the recovery of VMs and applications according to the predefined recovery plan. Administrators can initiate failover operations manually through the SRM interface or configure automatic failover policies based on predefined conditions such as network connectivity loss or storage failure. Throughout the failover process, SRM provides visibility into recovery progress, status updates, and post-failover tasks, allowing administrators to monitor and manage recovery operations effectively. VMware vSphere Replication and Site Recovery Manager are essential components of a comprehensive DR strategy, providing organizations with the tools and capabilities to replicate, recover, and restore virtualized workloads in the event of a disaster or outage. By leveraging vSphere Replication's asynchronous replication technology and SRM's automated orchestration capabilities, organizations can minimize downtime, improve recovery times, and ensure business continuity in the face of unforeseen disruptions.*

Monitoring performance metrics in vSphere is crucial for ensuring the health, stability, and efficiency of virtualized environments. vSphere provides a comprehensive set of tools and features for monitoring various aspects of virtual infrastructure, including CPU, memory, storage, and network utilization, as well as VM and host performance metrics. One of the primary tools for monitoring performance in vSphere is vCenter Server, which serves as the centralized management platform for virtualized environments. Within vCenter Server, administrators can access performance charts and graphs that provide real-time and historical data on resource utilization and performance trends. These performance charts allow administrators to monitor CPU usage, memory usage, disk I/O, network throughput, and other key metrics for individual VMs, hosts, clusters, and datastores. To access performance charts in vCenter Server, administrators can navigate to the "Monitor" tab and select the "Performance" submenu. From there, they can choose the desired object (VM, host, cluster, or datastore) and specify the performance metrics to display. Administrators can also customize performance charts by adjusting the time range, sampling interval, and chart options to focus on specific metrics or time periods. In addition to vCenter Server, administrators can use command-line tools such as esxtop and resxtop to monitor performance metrics directly from ESXi hosts. Esxtop is a powerful command-line utility that provides real-time monitoring of CPU, memory, disk, and network usage at the host level. To launch esxtop, administrators can SSH into the ESXi host and run the "esxtop" command. This opens the esxtop interface, which displays a variety of performance metrics organized into different views, including CPU, memory, disk, network, and virtual machine statistics. Within esxtop, administrators can navigate between different views using the function keys (F1-F12) and customize the display to focus on specific metrics or resource groups. Resxtop is a remote version of esxtop that can be run from a remote system to monitor performance metrics across multiple ESXi hosts. To use resxtop, administrators can SSH into a remote ESXi host and run the "resxtop" command with the appropriate options to connect to the target ESXi host and display performance metrics in real-time. Resxtop provides similar functionality to esxtop but allows administrators to monitor performance across multiple hosts from a single interface. In addition to vCenter Server and command-line tools, administrators can also use third-party monitoring solutions and plugins to extend vSphere's monitoring capabilities. These solutions provide advanced features such as predictive analytics, anomaly detection, and integration with other IT management tools. By leveraging these tools, administrators can gain deeper insights into the performance of their virtual infrastructure and proactively identify and address potential issues before they impact the business. Overall, monitoring performance metrics in vSphere is essential for maintaining the health, efficiency, and reliability of virtualized environments. Whether using vCenter Server, command-line tools, or third-party solutions, administrators can leverage a variety of tools and techniques to monitor performance and ensure optimal operation of their virtual infrastructure.

Troubleshooting performance issues and bottlenecks in an IT environment is a critical aspect of maintaining optimal system performance and ensuring the smooth operation of business-critical applications. When performance issues arise, it's essential to quickly identify the root cause and take corrective action to minimize downtime and prevent further impact on users and operations. One common approach to troubleshooting performance issues is to use monitoring tools to gather data on system performance and identify areas of concern.

In VMware vSphere environments, administrators can use tools such as vCenter Server, esxtop, and Performance Charts to monitor CPU, memory, disk, and network utilization and identify potential bottlenecks. In vCenter Server, administrators can access performance charts and graphs that provide real-time and historical data on resource utilization, allowing them to identify trends and patterns that may indicate performance issues. By analyzing performance metrics such as CPU usage, memory usage, disk latency, and network throughput, administrators can pinpoint areas of contention and prioritize troubleshooting efforts. Esxtop is a command-line utility that provides real-time monitoring of system performance at the host level. Administrators can use esxtop to view CPU, memory, disk, and network statistics and identify resource-intensive processes or VMs that may be causing performance issues. By monitoring metrics such as %RDY (CPU Ready), %WAIT (Disk Wait), and %SWPWT (Memory Swap Wait), administrators can identify bottlenecks and take appropriate action to alleviate them. Performance troubleshooting in vSphere often involves analyzing performance metrics across multiple layers of the virtual infrastructure, including VMs, hosts, clusters, and datastores. Administrators may need to correlate performance data from different sources to identify the underlying cause of performance issues *accurately. For example, a high CPU usage on a VM may be caused by resource contention at the host level, indicating the need to rebalance VM workloads or add additional host resources. Similarly, a high disk latency on a datastore may be caused by storage congestion or misconfigurations, requiring investigation into storage performance and configuration settings. In addition to monitoring tools, administrators can use diagnostic techniques such as log analysis and performance testing to troubleshoot performance issues. Log analysis involves reviewing system logs and error messages to identify any anomalies or issues that may be impacting performance. By analyzing log files from vSphere components such as ESXi hosts, vCenter Server, and VMs, administrators can identify errors, warnings, and other indicators of system health and performance. Performance testing involves running synthetic workloads or stress tests to simulate real-world usage scenarios and identify potential performance bottlenecks. By subjecting the system to increased load and monitoring performance metrics in real-time, administrators can identify performance limitations and evaluate the effectiveness of potential solutions. When troubleshooting performance issues, it's essential to follow a systematic approach and gather as much data as possible to accurately diagnose the problem. This may involve collecting performance data over time, correlating data from multiple sources, and testing different hypotheses to isolate the root cause. By leveraging monitoring tools, diagnostic techniques, and best practices, administrators can effectively troubleshoot performance issues and maintain optimal system performance in vSphere environments.*

VMware vRealize Automation is a powerful cloud automation platform that enables organizations to automate the deployment and management of their IT infrastructure and applications. It provides self-service capabilities for users to request and provision virtual machines, containers, and other resources from a centralized portal, streamlining the process of deploying and managing IT services. With vRealize Automation, organizations can accelerate service delivery, improve resource utilization, and enhance agility and flexibility in their IT operations. One of the key features of vRealize Automation is its ability to automate the provisioning of virtualized infrastructure, including virtual machines, networks, and storage resources. Using vRealize Automation's graphical user interface (GUI) or command-line interface (CLI), administrators can create blueprints that define the configuration and specifications of IT services, such as virtual machine templates, networking configurations, and security policies. These blueprints can then be published to the vRealize Automation catalog, where users can easily request and deploy them with a few clicks. By standardizing and automating the provisioning process, organizations can reduce the time and effort required to deploy new IT services and ensure consistency and compliance across their infrastructure. Another key capability of vRealize Automation is its integration with cloud platforms and third-party tools, allowing organizations to leverage existing investments and extend their automation capabilities across hybrid and multi-cloud environments. vRealize Automation provides out-of-the-box integrations with VMware vSphere, VMware NSX, VMware vSAN, and other VMware products, enabling seamless automation of VMware-based infrastructure. Additionally, vRealize Automation offers integration with public cloud platforms such as Amazon Web Services (AWS), Microsoft Azure, and Google Cloud Platform (GCP), allowing organizations to automate the deployment and management of cloud-native services and resources. By integrating with existing tools and platforms, vRealize Automation enables organizations to leverage their existing investments and infrastructure while gaining the benefits of automation and self-service provisioning. In addition to provisioning and managing infrastructure resources, vRealize Automation also provides advanced capabilities for orchestrating and automating complex IT processes and workflows. Using vRealize Automation's visual workflow designer, administrators can create custom automation workflows that integrate with third-party systems and tools, such as service desks, ticketing systems, and configuration management databases (CMDBs). These workflows can automate tasks such as application deployment, configuration management, and compliance auditing, enabling organizations to streamline their IT operations and improve efficiency and agility. With vRealize Automation, organizations can also enforce governance and compliance policies across their infrastructure and applications. Using role-based access control (RBAC) and policy-based governance, administrators can define granular access controls and enforce compliance policies to ensure that resources are provisioned and managed according to organizational policies and standards. By centralizing governance and compliance management, vRealize Automation helps organizations reduce risk, improve security, and maintain regulatory compliance across their IT environment. In summary, VMware vRealize Automation is a comprehensive cloud automation platform that enables organizations to automate the deployment and management of their IT infrastructure and applications. By providing self-service provisioning, integration with existing tools and platforms, advanced automation capabilities, and governance and compliance features, vRealize Automation empowers organizations to accelerate service delivery, improve agility and efficiency, and enhance the overall user experience. VMware vRealize Orchestrator (vRO) is a powerful automation tool that enables organizations to orchestrate complex workflows and automate IT processes across their infrastructure. With vRO, organizations can streamline repetitive tasks, improve operational efficiency, and enhance agility in their IT operations. One of the key features of vRealize Orchestrator is its extensive library of pre-built workflows and actions, which provide out-of-the-box automation capabilities for common IT tasks and processes. Using vRO's graphical workflow editor, administrators can easily drag and drop workflow elements to create custom automation workflows that automate tasks such as provisioning virtual machines, configuring network settings, and managing storage resources. These workflows can be customized to meet the specific needs of an organization and can be reused across different environments, saving time and effort in the automation process. In addition to its built-in workflow library, vRealize Orchestrator also supports integration with third-party systems and tools, allowing organizations to leverage existing investments and extend their automation capabilities. Using vRO's extensive library of plugins and integrations, administrators can automate tasks across a wide range of IT systems and applications, including virtualization platforms, cloud services, databases, and more. By integrating with third-party systems, vRealize Orchestrator enables organizations to create end-to-end automation workflows that span multiple systems and processes, enabling seamless automation of complex IT tasks. One of the key benefits of vRealize Orchestrator is its flexibility and extensibility, which allow organizations to tailor automation workflows to their unique requirements. Using vRO's JavaScript-based scripting engine, administrators can write custom scripts and functions to extend the functionality of their automation workflows and integrate with external systems and APIs. This flexibility enables organizations to automate a wide range of tasks and processes, from simple administrative tasks to complex business processes. For example, administrators can use vRO to automate the provisioning of virtual machines in VMware vSphere, the deployment of applications in cloud environments, or the integration of IT systems with external monitoring and alerting tools. In addition to its graphical workflow editor and scripting engine, vRealize Orchestrator also provides a command-line interface (CLI) for automating tasks and workflows from the command line. Using the vRO CLI, administrators can execute workflows, retrieve workflow results, and manage vRO resources from a command-line interface, enabling streamlined automation of routine tasks and processes. The vRO CLI provides a set of commands for interacting with vRO servers, including commands for deploying and configuring workflows, managing plugins and packages, and monitoring workflow execution. By leveraging the vRO CLI, administrators can automate repetitive tasks, streamline their workflow development process, and integrate vRealize Orchestrator into their existing automation workflows and toolchains. In summary, VMware vRealize Orchestrator is a powerful automation tool that enables organizations to orchestrate complex workflows and automate IT processes across their infrastructure. With its graphical workflow editor, scripting engine, and command-line interface, vRO provides flexible and extensible automation capabilities that help organizations improve operational efficiency, enhance agility, and accelerate service delivery. Whether automating simple administrative tasks or orchestrating complex business processes, vRealize Orchestrator empowers organizations to streamline their IT operations and drive innovation.

VMware Cloud Foundation (VCF) is a comprehensive software-defined data center (SDDC) platform that integrates compute, storage, networking, and management services into a single unified platform. This platform is designed to simplify the deployment, management, and operations of hybrid cloud infrastructures, enabling organizations to accelerate their digital transformation initiatives. At the core of VMware Cloud Foundation is the VMware Software Stack, which includes VMware vSphere for virtualization, VMware vSAN for storage, and VMware NSX for networking. These components are tightly integrated and pre-configured to provide a consistent and reliable infrastructure foundation for running traditional and modern applications across private, public, and hybrid cloud environments. One of the key features of VMware Cloud Foundation is its ability to automate the deployment and lifecycle management of the entire SDDC stack. Using VMware Cloud Builder, administrators can quickly deploy a standardized VMware Cloud Foundation environment with just *a few clicks. This automated deployment process ensures consistency and reduces the time and effort required to provision and configure infrastructure resources. Additionally, VMware Cloud Foundation includes VMware Lifecycle Manager (VLCM), which automates the lifecycle management of the SDDC stack, including patching, upgrading, and scaling operations. With VLCM, administrators can easily apply software updates and patches to the entire SDDC stack in a controlled and non-disruptive manner, ensuring the security and stability of the infrastructure. VMware Cloud Foundation also provides built-in support for hybrid cloud connectivity, allowing organizations to seamlessly extend their on-premises SDDC environments to public cloud providers such as VMware Cloud on AWS, Microsoft Azure, and Google Cloud Platform. This enables organizations to leverage the scalability and agility of public cloud services while maintaining control and consistency across their hybrid cloud environments. Another key feature of VMware Cloud Foundation is its support for cloud-native applications and containerized workloads. With native integration with Kubernetes and VMware Tanzu, organizations can deploy and manage containerized applications alongside traditional virtual machine workloads on the same infrastructure platform. This enables organizations to modernize their application development and delivery processes while leveraging existing infrastructure investments. VMware Cloud Foundation also provides advanced networking and security capabilities through integration with VMware NSX. With NSX, organizations can create virtual networks, micro-segmentation policies, and firewall rules to secure their applications and data across the entire SDDC stack. This helps organizations protect against advanced threats and comply with regulatory requirements. In addition to its core features, VMware Cloud Foundation offers a range of additional services and integrations to extend the capabilities of the platform. These include VMware vRealize Suite for cloud management and automation, VMware HCX for workload migration and mobility, and VMware Cloud Director for multi-tenancy and self-service provisioning. By leveraging these additional services, organizations can further optimize their cloud infrastructure and accelerate their digital transformation journey. In summary, VMware Cloud Foundation is a comprehensive SDDC platform that provides a unified infrastructure foundation for running traditional and modern applications across hybrid cloud environments. With its automated deployment and lifecycle management capabilities, built-in support for hybrid cloud connectivity, and advanced networking and security features, VMware Cloud Foundation enables organizations to streamline their IT operations, improve agility, and accelerate innovation. Whether deploying traditional workloads, modernizing applications, or extending to the cloud, VMware Cloud Foundation provides the flexibility and scalability that organizations need to succeed in today's digital world.*

VMware HCX, or Hybrid Cloud Extension, is a powerful solution designed to facilitate seamless cloud migrations and workload mobility between on-premises environments and public cloud platforms. This innovative technology enables organizations to overcome the complexities and challenges associated with migrating workloads to the cloud by providing a unified platform for migration, interconnectivity, and workload mobility. With VMware HCX, organizations can seamlessly extend their on-premises VMware-based infrastructure to the cloud, enabling them to leverage the scalability, agility, and cost-effectiveness of public cloud services while maintaining operational consistency and control. One of the key features of VMware HCX is its ability to provide secure and high-performance connectivity between on-premises data centers and public cloud environments. By leveraging advanced networking technologies such as Layer 2 VPN and WAN optimization, VMware HCX enables organizations to establish a seamless and resilient network connection between their on-premises infrastructure and their chosen public cloud provider. This ensures that workloads can be migrated to the cloud without disruption to ongoing operations and without compromising security or performance. In addition to providing secure connectivity, VMware HCX also offers a range of migration capabilities to simplify the process of migrating workloads to the cloud. One such capability is live migration, which enables organizations to move virtual machines (VMs) from their on-premises environment to the cloud with minimal downtime or disruption. Using the VMware HCX vMotion technology, organizations can migrate VMs between on-premises and cloud environments while they are still running, ensuring continuous availability and minimal impact on end users. Another key migration capability provided by VMware HCX is bulk migration, which enables organizations to migrate large numbers of VMs to the cloud in a fast and efficient manner. By leveraging technologies such as VMware HCX Bulk Migration, organizations can automate the *migration process and accelerate time-to-value, enabling them to realize the benefits of cloud migration more quickly and easily. VMware HCX also provides advanced workload mobility capabilities to enable organizations to move workloads between on-premises and cloud environments as needed. With features such as stretch clustering and workload mobility, organizations can dynamically move workloads between different infrastructure environments based on factors such as performance, cost, and resource availability. This enables organizations to optimize their infrastructure resources and ensure that workloads are running in the most efficient and cost-effective environment at all times. Additionally, VMware HCX provides a range of management and monitoring capabilities to enable organizations to track and manage their cloud migrations effectively. Using the VMware HCX Control Plane, organizations can monitor the status of their migrations, track performance metrics, and troubleshoot issues as they arise. This enables organizations to ensure that their cloud migrations are proceeding smoothly and according to plan, minimizing the risk of disruption to their business operations. In summary, VMware HCX is a powerful solution for seamless cloud migrations and workload mobility, enabling organizations to overcome the complexities and challenges associated with migrating workloads to the cloud. By providing secure connectivity, advanced migration capabilities, and workload mobility features, VMware HCX enables organizations to realize the benefits of cloud computing while maintaining operational consistency and control. Whether migrating workloads to the cloud, extending on-premises infrastructure to the cloud, or dynamically moving workloads between different environments, VMware HCX provides the flexibility, scalability, and performance that organizations need to succeed in today's hybrid cloud world.*

BOOK 4
NAVIGATING NAVISITE
EXPERT TACTICS FOR SEAMLESS CLOUD INTEGRATION

ROB BOTWRIGHT

The history and evolution of NaviSite trace back to its inception in the late 1990s, during the dot-com boom, when the demand for internet-based services and hosting solutions began to surge. NaviSite was founded in 1997 with the vision of providing managed hosting, cloud services, and application management solutions to businesses seeking to establish an online presence and leverage the power of the internet for their operations. Initially, NaviSite focused on offering colocation services, providing businesses with the infrastructure and support they needed to host their websites and applications in secure data center facilities. As the internet landscape continued to evolve, NaviSite expanded its service offerings to meet the growing demands of its customers and the changing technology landscape. In the early 2000s, NaviSite began to transition from a pure colocation provider to a managed hosting provider, offering a broader range of services, including managed servers, network services, and security solutions. This shift allowed NaviSite to cater to the needs of businesses that required more comprehensive managed hosting solutions, including proactive monitoring, maintenance, and support for their IT infrastructure. With the rise of cloud computing in the late 2000s, NaviSite recognized the potential of cloud technologies to transform the way businesses deploy and manage their IT resources. In response, NaviSite began to invest heavily in cloud infrastructure and services, developing its own cloud platform and partnering with leading cloud providers such as Amazon Web Services (AWS), Microsoft Azure, and VMware to offer a comprehensive suite of cloud services to its customers. This strategic shift positioned NaviSite as a leading provider of cloud services, enabling businesses to leverage the scalability, flexibility, and cost-effectiveness of cloud computing for their IT needs. In 2011, NaviSite was acquired by Time Warner Cable, further enhancing its capabilities and resources to serve the evolving needs of its customers. Under Time Warner Cable's ownership, NaviSite continued to expand its service offerings and geographic footprint, establishing itself as a trusted partner for businesses seeking to navigate the complexities of the digital age. In 2016, Time Warner Cable was acquired by Charter Communications, further solidifying NaviSite's position as a leading provider of managed hosting and cloud services. Today, NaviSite continues to innovate and evolve, offering a comprehensive portfolio of solutions to help businesses thrive in an increasingly digital world. From managed hosting and cloud services to cybersecurity and digital transformation consulting, NaviSite remains committed to delivering exceptional value and service to its customers, empowering them to achieve their business objectives and stay ahead of the competition.

The core principles and values of NaviSite embody its commitment to excellence, integrity, and customer satisfaction. At the heart of NaviSite's philosophy is a dedication to delivering innovative solutions that empower businesses to succeed in the digital age. Central to NaviSite's values is a relentless focus on customer success, ensuring that every interaction and engagement is driven by the goal of helping customers achieve their objectives and overcome their challenges. This customer-centric approach is reflected in NaviSite's commitment to understanding the unique needs and requirements of each customer and tailoring solutions that address their specific challenges and goals. One of the key principles that guides NaviSite's operations is a commitment to excellence in everything it does. From the *quality of its services and solutions to the expertise of its team members, NaviSite strives for excellence in every aspect of its business. This commitment to excellence is evident in NaviSite's rigorous quality assurance processes, which ensure that its services meet the highest standards of performance, reliability, and security. Moreover, NaviSite's dedication to excellence extends to its ongoing investment in research and development, enabling it to stay at the forefront of technological innovation and deliver cutting-edge solutions that drive business value. Integrity is another core value that lies at the foundation of NaviSite's culture. NaviSite is committed to conducting its business with honesty, transparency, and ethical integrity at all times. This commitment to integrity is reflected in NaviSite's adherence to the highest ethical standards in its interactions with customers, partners, and employees. Furthermore, NaviSite places a strong emphasis on trust and accountability, ensuring that it always acts in the best interests of its customers and maintains the trust and confidence they place in its services. Collaboration is a fundamental principle that underpins NaviSite's approach to business. NaviSite recognizes that success is often achieved through collaboration and partnership, both internally within its organization and externally with its customers and partners. NaviSite fosters a culture of collaboration, teamwork, and mutual respect, encouraging open communication, knowledge sharing, and collaboration across teams and departments. This collaborative approach enables NaviSite to leverage the diverse skills, experiences, and perspectives of its team members to deliver innovative solutions and exceptional service to its customers. Additionally, NaviSite actively seeks out opportunities to collaborate with its customers and partners to co-create solutions that address their specific needs and challenges. By working closely with customers and partners, NaviSite is able to gain valuable insights into their businesses, identify opportunities for improvement, and develop tailored solutions that drive tangible results. Innovation is a core value that drives NaviSite's continued growth and success. NaviSite is committed to fostering a culture of innovation and entrepreneurship, empowering its employees to think creatively, challenge the status quo, and pursue bold ideas that push the boundaries of what is possible. NaviSite encourages experimentation, risk-taking, and continuous learning, recognizing that innovation often requires taking calculated risks and learning from* both successes and failures. This commitment to innovation is evident in NaviSite's ongoing investment in research and development, as well as its strategic partnerships with leading technology providers and startups. By embracing innovation, NaviSite is able to anticipate emerging trends, capitalize on new opportunities, and deliver solutions that drive business value for its customers. Accountability is a fundamental principle that governs NaviSite's operations and decision-making processes. NaviSite holds itself accountable for delivering results and upholding the highest standards of performance, quality, and integrity. This commitment to accountability is reflected in NaviSite's rigorous performance metrics and Key Performance Indicators (KPIs), which are used to track progress, measure success, and drive continuous improvement. Furthermore, NaviSite encourages a culture of personal responsibility and ownership, empowering its employees to take initiative, make decisions, and take ownership of their work. By fostering a culture of accountability, NaviSite ensures that its employees are fully engaged, motivated, and committed to delivering exceptional service and value to its customers. Adaptability is a core value that enables NaviSite to thrive in an ever-changing and dynamic *business environment. NaviSite recognizes that success often requires the ability to adapt to changing market conditions, customer needs, and technological advancements. Therefore, NaviSite places a strong emphasis on agility, flexibility, and responsiveness, ensuring that it can quickly pivot and adjust its strategies, plans, and operations to meet evolving challenges and seize new opportunities. This commitment to adaptability is reflected in NaviSite's willingness to embrace change, experiment with new ideas, and continuously iterate and improve its processes and practices. By remaining agile and adaptable, NaviSite is able to stay ahead of the curve, anticipate market trends, and proactively address emerging challenges, ensuring that it can continue to deliver value and innovation to its customers for years to come.*

NaviSite's cloud services portfolio encompasses a comprehensive range of solutions designed to meet the diverse needs of businesses in the digital age. At the core of NaviSite's cloud offerings is its Infrastructure as a Service (IaaS) platform, which provides businesses with scalable, flexible, and reliable infrastructure resources on demand. Leveraging the power of virtualization and automation, NaviSite's IaaS platform enables businesses to deploy and manage virtual servers, storage, and networking resources in the cloud, allowing them to rapidly provision and scale infrastructure to support their evolving business needs. One of the key advantages of NaviSite's IaaS platform is its ability to deliver enterprise-grade performance, reliability, and security, ensuring that businesses can run their mission-critical workloads with confidence in the cloud. Moreover, NaviSite's IaaS platform is highly customizable, allowing businesses to tailor their infrastructure configurations to meet their specific requirements and preferences. Another cornerstone of NaviSite's cloud services portfolio is its Platform as a Service (PaaS) offerings, which provide businesses with a comprehensive suite of tools and services for developing, deploying, and managing cloud-native applications. NaviSite's PaaS solutions include a wide range of services, such as application hosting, database management, developer tools, and analytics capabilities, enabling businesses to build and run modern, scalable, and resilient applications in the cloud. With NaviSite's PaaS offerings, businesses can accelerate their application development lifecycle, streamline their operations, and drive innovation, all while reducing the complexity and cost of managing their application infrastructure. Additionally, NaviSite's PaaS solutions are designed to integrate seamlessly with other cloud services and third-party tools, providing businesses with the flexibility and agility they need to build and deploy applications in a hybrid or multi-cloud environment. In addition to its IaaS and PaaS offerings, NaviSite also provides a comprehensive suite of Software as a Service (SaaS) solutions, which enable businesses to access and utilize a wide range of business-critical applications and services on a subscription basis. NaviSite's SaaS offerings cover a broad spectrum of applications, including productivity tools, collaboration software, customer relationship management

(CRM) systems, enterprise resource planning (ERP) solutions, and more, empowering businesses to streamline their operations, enhance their productivity, and drive better business outcomes. By leveraging NaviSite's SaaS solutions, businesses can avoid the complexity and overhead of managing on-premises software deployments, while benefiting from the scalability, reliability, and security of cloud-based applications. Furthermore, NaviSite's SaaS offerings are continuously updated and enhanced by NaviSite's team of experts, ensuring that businesses always have access to the latest features, capabilities, and security enhancements. In addition to its core cloud services offerings, NaviSite also provides a wide range of managed services to help businesses optimize their cloud environments, maximize their return on investment, and mitigate risks. NaviSite's managed services offerings include cloud migration and onboarding services, cloud optimization and cost management services, security and compliance services, monitoring and performance management services, and more, enabling businesses to offload the day-to-day management and maintenance of their cloud infrastructure to NaviSite's team of experts. By leveraging NaviSite's managed services, businesses can free up their internal IT resources

to focus on strategic initiatives, innovation, and driving business value, while NaviSite handles the operational aspects of managing their cloud environments. Moreover, NaviSite's managed services are backed by industry-leading service level agreements (SLAs) and 24/7 support, ensuring that businesses have access to the expertise and assistance they need, whenever they need it. Overall, NaviSite's cloud services portfolio offers businesses a comprehensive suite of solutions to help them harness the power of the cloud, drive innovation, and achieve their business objectives in the digital age. Whether businesses are looking to modernize their infrastructure, develop and deploy cloud-native applications, or access and utilize business-critical software applications, NaviSite has the expertise, experience, and capabilities to help them succeed in the cloud.
NaviSite offers a variety of industry-specific solutions tailored to meet the unique needs and challenges of different sectors. For instance, in the healthcare industry, NaviSite provides compliant cloud solutions designed to safeguard sensitive patient data and ensure HIPAA compliance. These solutions include secure hosting environments, data encryption, access controls, and regular audits to maintain regulatory compliance.

Moreover, NaviSite's healthcare solutions offer scalability and flexibility to support the growing demands of healthcare organizations while maintaining high levels of security and performance. Similarly, in the financial services sector, NaviSite delivers cloud solutions that address stringent regulatory requirements such as PCI DSS and SOC compliance. These solutions include secure data storage, encryption, access controls, and real-time monitoring to protect sensitive financial data and ensure compliance with industry regulations. Additionally, NaviSite's financial services solutions offer high availability, disaster recovery, and business continuity capabilities to minimize downtime and ensure uninterrupted operations. In the retail industry, NaviSite offers e-commerce solutions that enable retailers to build and manage online stores efficiently. These solutions include scalable infrastructure, content delivery networks (CDNs), and caching mechanisms to deliver fast and reliable shopping experiences for customers. Furthermore, NaviSite's e-commerce solutions integrate with popular e-commerce platforms such as Magento, WooCommerce, and Shopify, allowing retailers to leverage existing tools and workflows. In the manufacturing sector, NaviSite provides cloud solutions that support digital transformation initiatives and enhance operational efficiency. These solutions include IoT platforms, predictive analytics, and supply chain management tools to optimize production processes, improve product quality, and reduce costs. Moreover, NaviSite's manufacturing solutions offer real-time visibility into factory operations, enabling manufacturers to make data-driven decisions and respond quickly to changing market conditions. In the media and entertainment industry, NaviSite offers cloud solutions that enable content creators to store, manage, and distribute digital assets efficiently. These solutions include media asset management systems, video transcoding services, and content delivery networks (CDNs) to streamline content production workflows and deliver high-quality multimedia experiences to audiences worldwide. Additionally, NaviSite's media and entertainment solutions provide scalability and flexibility to accommodate the varying demands of media companies and adapt to evolving technologies and consumption trends. In the education sector, NaviSite offers cloud solutions that support online learning initiatives and enhance collaboration among students, educators, and administrators. These solutions include learning management systems (LMS), virtual classrooms, and *collaboration tools to facilitate remote learning, course delivery, and student engagement. Furthermore, NaviSite's education solutions integrate with existing academic systems and support interoperability standards such as LTI and IMS Global, enabling seamless integration with other educational applications and services. Overall, NaviSite's industry solutions empower organizations across various sectors to leverage the full potential of cloud technology and achieve their business objectives in a rapidly evolving digital landscape. Whether organizations are looking to enhance patient care, improve financial security, optimize retail operations, streamline manufacturing processes, deliver compelling media experiences, or transform education delivery, NaviSite has the expertise, experience, and solutions to help them succeed.*

When planning for NaviSite Cloud deployment, several key considerations must be taken into account to ensure a successful implementation. First and foremost, organizations need to assess their current IT infrastructure, including hardware, software, and networking components, to determine the scope of the migration to the cloud. This assessment should include an inventory of existing applications, databases, and workloads, as well as an analysis of performance, security, and compliance requirements. Once the current state has been assessed, organizations can begin to define their cloud migration strategy, outlining goals, timelines, and resource requirements. This strategy should consider factors such as workload compatibility, data residency requirements, and cost implications to ensure a smooth transition to the cloud. Additionally, organizations should carefully evaluate their application portfolio to identify which workloads are suitable for migration to the cloud and which may require refactoring or rearchitecting. This evaluation should take into account factors such as *application dependencies, performance requirements, and regulatory compliance. Furthermore, organizations should consider the architectural principles and best practices recommended by NaviSite when designing their cloud environment. These principles include scalability, reliability, security, and performance optimization, which are essential for building a robust and resilient cloud infrastructure. Additionally, organizations should consider the use of cloud-native services and technologies, such as containers, serverless computing, and microservices architecture, to take full advantage of the benefits offered by the cloud. When it comes to network architecture, organizations should design a network topology that provides high availability, low latency, and secure connectivity to NaviSite Cloud resources. This may involve deploying virtual private networks (VPNs), firewalls, and load balancers to ensure optimal performance and security. Moreover, organizations should consider implementing hybrid cloud or multi-cloud architectures to leverage existing on-premises infrastructure while taking advantage of the scalability and flexibility of the cloud. This may involve connecting on-premises data centers to NaviSite Cloud using dedicated connections or VPN tunnels, enabling seamless integration and workload mobility between environments. Additionally, organizations should consider implementing disaster recovery and business continuity strategies to ensure data protection and availability in the event of unforeseen disruptions. This may involve replicating data and workloads across multiple geographic regions or data centers, implementing automated failover mechanisms, and regularly testing disaster recovery plans to ensure readiness. Furthermore, organizations should consider the cost implications of their cloud architecture and design solutions that optimize cost efficiency while meeting performance and scalability requirements. This may involve implementing cost management tools and practices, such as usage monitoring, resource tagging, and rightsizing, to identify cost-saving opportunities and optimize cloud spending. Overall, careful planning and thoughtful architecture design are critical for ensuring a successful NaviSite Cloud deployment. By considering factors such as workload compatibility, application architecture, network topology, and cost optimization, organizations can build a cloud environment that meets their business needs and delivers value over the long term.*

Designing scalable and resilient cloud solutions is crucial for organizations looking to leverage the full potential of cloud computing while ensuring high availability, performance, and reliability. To achieve this, several key principles and best practices must be followed throughout the design process. One fundamental aspect of designing scalable and resilient cloud solutions is understanding the principles of cloud architecture, including elasticity, fault tolerance, and distributed computing. These principles form the foundation for building cloud-native applications and infrastructure that can dynamically scale in response to changing workloads and withstand failures without impacting service availability. When designing cloud solutions, organizations should prioritize modular and loosely coupled architectures that enable components to scale independently and minimize dependencies. This allows for greater flexibility and agility in responding to evolving business requirements and traffic patterns. Moreover, organizations should leverage managed services and serverless computing platforms to offload operational overhead and focus on building core business logic. Platforms like AWS Lambda, Google Cloud Functions, and Azure Functions enable developers to write and deploy code without provisioning or managing servers, thereby reducing complexity and improving scalability. Additionally, organizations should adopt microservices architecture to break down monolithic applications into smaller, more manageable services that can be independently deployed, scaled, and maintained. This enables teams to iterate faster, release new features more frequently, and scale components horizontally to handle increased demand. In terms of infrastructure design, organizations should leverage cloud-native services and managed databases to offload administrative tasks and improve scalability and reliability. Platforms like Amazon RDS, Google Cloud SQL, and Azure Database provide fully managed database solutions with built-in scalability, automated backups, and high availability. Furthermore, organizations should implement distributed caching and content delivery networks (CDNs) to improve performance and reduce latency for global users. Services like Amazon ElastiCache, Google Cloud Memorystore, and Azure Cache for Redis enable organizations to cache frequently accessed data and serve content from edge locations closer to end-users, resulting in faster response times and improved user experience. When designing for scalability and resilience, it's essential to consider fault tolerance and disaster recovery strategies to mitigate the impact of hardware failures, network outages, and other disruptions. Organizations should implement multi-region deployments, data replication, and automated failover mechanisms to ensure continuous availability and data integrity. Platforms like AWS Global Accelerator, Google Cloud Global Load Balancer, and Azure Traffic Manager enable organizations to distribute traffic across multiple regions and automatically reroute traffic in the event of a failure. Moreover, organizations should implement monitoring, alerting, and logging solutions to proactively identify issues, troubleshoot performance bottlenecks, and ensure system reliability. Platforms like AWS CloudWatch, Google Cloud Monitoring, and Azure Monitor provide comprehensive monitoring and observability capabilities, allowing organizations to track key performance metrics, set up alerts, and analyze logs to diagnose and resolve issues quickly. In summary, designing scalable and resilient cloud solutions requires a holistic approach that encompasses architecture design, infrastructure planning, and operational best practices. By following cloud-native principles, leveraging managed services, and implementing fault-

tolerant and disaster recovery strategies, organizations can build robust and reliable cloud environments that meet their business needs and drive innovation.

Hybrid cloud computing combines on-premises infrastructure with public and private cloud services to create a unified and flexible IT environment. This approach offers organizations the benefits of both worlds, allowing them to leverage the scalability and agility of the cloud while maintaining control over sensitive data and applications. One of the fundamental principles of hybrid cloud computing is interoperability, which enables seamless integration and data sharing between different cloud environments and on-premises infrastructure. This interoperability is facilitated by standards-based protocols and APIs that allow applications and services to communicate and exchange data across hybrid environments. Organizations can deploy hybrid cloud solutions for a variety of use cases, ranging from extending on-premises applications to the cloud to implementing disaster recovery and backup solutions. For example, organizations may choose to migrate legacy applications to the cloud to take advantage of modern infrastructure and services while preserving existing investments in on-premises systems. This approach enables organizations to modernize their IT infrastructure, improve scalability, and reduce operational costs. Additionally, hybrid cloud solutions are ideal for implementing disaster recovery and business continuity strategies. By replicating critical data and workloads to the cloud, organizations can ensure that their applications remain available in the event of a data center outage or other disaster. This approach provides a cost-effective alternative to traditional disaster recovery solutions, enabling organizations to maintain high availability without the need for expensive secondary data centers. Another common use case for hybrid cloud computing is bursty or unpredictable workloads. In many industries, such as retail, finance, and healthcare, organizations experience seasonal spikes in demand or periodic processing-intensive tasks. By leveraging the elastic scalability of the cloud, organizations can dynamically scale their infrastructure to handle these peak workloads while maintaining optimal performance and cost efficiency. Hybrid cloud solutions also enable organizations to address regulatory and compliance requirements by keeping sensitive data on-premises while leveraging the cloud for less sensitive workloads. This approach allows organizations to maintain control over data residency and privacy while taking advantage of cloud services for non-sensitive tasks such as development and testing. Moreover, hybrid cloud computing facilitates cloud *bursting, a technique that enables organizations to scale their on-premises infrastructure into the cloud during periods of peak demand. This approach allows organizations to seamlessly extend their capacity beyond the limitations of their on-premises data center, ensuring that they can meet customer demands without compromising performance or reliability. To deploy a hybrid cloud solution, organizations can use a variety of tools and technologies, including virtual private networks (VPNs), direct connections, and hybrid cloud management platforms. For example, AWS Direct Connect and Azure ExpressRoute provide dedicated network connections between on-premises data centers and cloud environments, enabling secure and high-speed data transfer. Additionally, hybrid cloud management platforms like VMware Cloud Foundation and Azure Arc enable organizations to manage and orchestrate workloads across multiple environments from a single interface. These platforms provide unified management, security, and governance capabilities, allowing organizations to maintain visibility and control over their hybrid infrastructure. In summary, hybrid cloud computing offers organizations the flexibility, scalability, and agility they need to meet the demands of today's digital economy while maintaining control over sensitive data and applications. By leveraging a combination of on-premises infrastructure and cloud* services, organizations can achieve cost savings, improve operational efficiency, and drive innovation. Whether it's extending on-premises applications to the cloud, implementing disaster recovery and backup solutions, or addressing regulatory and compliance requirements, hybrid cloud computing provides a versatile and powerful platform for modernizing IT infrastructure and driving business growth.

Integrating on-premises infrastructure with NaviSite Cloud involves connecting existing data centers, servers, and networks to NaviSite's cloud services to create a unified and hybrid IT environment. This integration enables organizations to leverage the scalability, agility, and cost-effectiveness of the cloud while maintaining control over their on-premises resources. One of the key technologies used to facilitate this integration is hybrid cloud networking, which allows organizations to establish secure and high-speed connections between their on-premises infrastructure and NaviSite's cloud environment. For example, organizations can use virtual private networks (VPNs) to establish encrypted tunnels over the public internet, connecting their on-premises data centers to NaviSite's cloud services. Additionally, organizations can use dedicated connections, such as AWS Direct Connect or Azure ExpressRoute, to establish private and high-bandwidth connections between their on-premises infrastructure and NaviSite's cloud environment. These dedicated connections provide predictable performance, low latency, and increased security compared to VPNs over the public internet. Once the network connectivity is established, organizations can begin migrating workloads and data to NaviSite's cloud environment using various migration tools and techniques. One common approach is to use NaviSite's migration services, which provide a suite of tools and expertise to help organizations plan, execute, and optimize their cloud migration projects. These services include discovery and assessment tools to identify workloads and dependencies, migration tools to facilitate the transfer of data and applications, and post-migration optimization tools to ensure that workloads are running efficiently in the cloud. Alternatively, organizations can use third-party migration tools, such as VMware vSphere Replication and Azure Site Recovery, to replicate and migrate virtual machines and applications from on-premises infrastructure to NaviSite's cloud environment. These tools enable organizations to automate the migration process, reduce downtime, and minimize the risk of data loss during migration. In addition to migrating workloads, organizations must also consider how to integrate their on-premises identity and access management systems with NaviSite's cloud services. This involves synchronizing user accounts, groups, and permissions between on-premises Active Directory or LDAP directories and NaviSite's cloud identity services, such as Azure Active Directory or AWS Identity and Access Management (IAM). Organizations can use tools like Azure AD Connect or AWS Directory Service to synchronize user identities between on-premises and cloud environments, ensuring a seamless and consistent user experience across both environments. Furthermore, organizations may need to extend their existing security policies and controls to NaviSite's cloud environment to ensure compliance and protect sensitive data. This involves configuring network security groups, firewalls, and encryption settings to restrict access to resources and protect data in transit and at rest. For example, organizations can use security groups and access control lists (ACLs) to define rules that allow or deny traffic between on-premises and cloud environments based on IP addresses, ports, and protocols. Additionally, organizations can encrypt data using TLS/SSL or IPsec VPN tunnels to secure communications between on-premises and cloud environments. Overall, integrating on-premises infrastructure with NaviSite Cloud requires careful planning, design, and execution to ensure a seamless and secure transition to the cloud. By *leveraging hybrid cloud networking, migration tools, and identity management services, organizations can unlock the full potential of NaviSite's cloud services while preserving their existing investments in on-premises infrastructure.*

Managing multiple clouds presents a unique set of challenges and requires robust solutions to ensure seamless operation and optimal performance across diverse cloud environments. One of the primary challenges in multi-cloud management is the complexity introduced by the use of multiple cloud providers, each with its own set of services, APIs, and management interfaces. This complexity can lead to issues such as vendor lock-in, interoperability problems, and difficulty in maintaining consistent governance and compliance across clouds. To address these challenges, organizations can adopt a multi-cloud management platform that provides a unified interface for managing resources and workloads across multiple cloud environments. These platforms, such as VMware CloudHealth, Microsoft Azure Arc, or Google Anthos, enable organizations to centrally manage and monitor their cloud resources, regardless of the underlying cloud provider. They offer features such as centralized billing and cost management, resource provisioning and orchestration, and policy-based governance and compliance. Additionally, multi-cloud management platforms provide visibility and insights into cloud usage, performance, and security, allowing organizations to optimize resource utilization, identify cost savings opportunities, and mitigate security risks. Another challenge in multi-cloud management is ensuring consistent security and compliance posture across diverse cloud environments. With each cloud provider having its own set of security controls and compliance standards, organizations may struggle to enforce consistent security policies and ensure regulatory compliance across multiple clouds. To overcome this challenge, organizations can implement cloud security solutions that provide centralized visibility, control, and automation of security policies and compliance requirements across multi-cloud environments. These solutions, such as cloud security posture management (CSPM) tools and cloud compliance frameworks, enable organizations to define and enforce security policies, monitor compliance with regulatory standards, and remediate security issues in real-time. Moreover, organizations can leverage cloud-native security services offered by cloud providers, such as AWS Security Hub, Azure Security Center, or Google Cloud Security Command Center, to gain insights into security threats and vulnerabilities across their multi-cloud environments. Another critical aspect of multi-cloud management is optimizing costs and maximizing ROI across multiple cloud providers. Without proper cost management and optimization strategies, organizations may face cost overruns, budget constraints, and inefficient resource utilization in their multi-cloud environments. To address these challenges, organizations can implement cloud cost management solutions that provide visibility into cloud spending, identify cost-saving opportunities, and automate cost optimization actions.

These solutions, such as cloud cost analytics platforms and cost allocation tools, enable organizations to track cloud spending by workload, department, or project, identify unused or underutilized resources, and implement cost-saving measures such as rightsizing instances, leveraging reserved instances, or adopting spot instances. Additionally, organizations can use cloud governance frameworks and policies to enforce budget controls, monitor spending trends, and align cloud spending with business objectives. Overall, multi-cloud management requires a comprehensive approach that addresses the complexity, security, and cost challenges inherent in managing multiple cloud environments. By adopting multi-cloud management platforms, implementing cloud security solutions, and optimizing costs across diverse cloud environments, organizations can unlock the full potential of multi-cloud architectures and drive innovation and agility in their digital transformation journey.

NaviSite offers a comprehensive approach to multi-cloud orchestration, enabling organizations to efficiently manage and orchestrate workloads across diverse cloud environments. Central to NaviSite's approach is the use of automation and orchestration tools to streamline cloud management tasks and ensure consistency and reliability across multi-cloud deployments. One key aspect of NaviSite's multi-cloud orchestration strategy is the use of Infrastructure as Code (IaC) principles, which allow organizations to define and provision cloud infrastructure using code-based templates and configurations. By adopting IaC tools such as Terraform or AWS CloudFormation, organizations can automate the deployment and configuration of cloud resources, ensuring consistency and repeatability across different cloud environments. Additionally, NaviSite leverages containerization technologies such as Docker and Kubernetes to enable portability and *scalability of applications across multi-cloud environments. By containerizing applications, organizations can package their applications and dependencies into lightweight, portable containers that can run consistently across any cloud platform. This approach enables organizations to achieve greater flexibility and agility in deploying and managing applications across hybrid and multi-cloud environments. Furthermore, NaviSite provides a unified management platform that offers centralized visibility and control over multi-cloud resources. This platform enables organizations to monitor and manage their cloud environments through a single pane of glass, simplifying operations and reducing complexity. With features such as centralized monitoring, logging, and alerting, organizations can gain insights into the performance, availability, and security of their multi-cloud deployments, allowing them to proactively identify and address issues before they impact business operations. Another key component of NaviSite's multi-cloud orchestration approach is the use of cloud-native services and APIs to integrate with various cloud providers. By leveraging cloud-native services such as AWS Lambda, Azure Functions, or Google Cloud Pub/Sub, organizations can build event-driven architectures that enable seamless integration* and interoperability between different cloud environments. This enables organizations to leverage the unique capabilities and features of each cloud provider while maintaining interoperability and portability across multi-cloud deployments. Moreover, NaviSite provides comprehensive security and compliance solutions to ensure the security and integrity of multi-cloud environments. By implementing security best practices such as identity and access management (IAM), encryption, and network segmentation, organizations can protect their sensitive data and applications from security threats and vulnerabilities. Additionally, NaviSite offers compliance automation tools and services that help organizations achieve and maintain compliance with regulatory standards such as PCI DSS, HIPAA, and GDPR. By automating compliance checks and audits, organizations can reduce the time and effort required to achieve and maintain compliance, allowing them to focus on driving business innovation and growth. In summary, NaviSite's approach to multi-cloud orchestration is built on automation, containerization, centralized management, and cloud-native integration, enabling organizations to efficiently manage and orchestrate workloads across diverse cloud environments while ensuring security, compliance, *and reliability. By adopting NaviSite's multi-cloud orchestration solutions, organizations can unlock the full potential of multi-cloud architectures and drive innovation and agility in their digital transformation journey.*

NaviSite's security framework and best practices are designed to ensure the confidentiality, integrity, and availability of data and resources across its cloud infrastructure. At the core of NaviSite's security framework is a defense-in-depth approach, which involves implementing multiple layers of security controls to protect against various threats and vulnerabilities. One key aspect of NaviSite's security framework is the use of identity and access management (IAM) policies to control access to resources. By defining IAM policies, organizations can specify who has access to specific resources and what actions they can perform. This helps prevent unauthorized access and ensures that only authorized users can access sensitive data and perform privileged actions. To create IAM policies in AWS, organizations can use the AWS Management Console or the AWS Command Line Interface (CLI). Using the AWS CLI, organizations can use the "aws iam create-policy" command to create a new IAM policy. For example, the following command creates a new IAM policy named "ExamplePolicy" with the specified permissions: aws iam create-policy --policy-name ExamplePolicy --policy-document file://example-policy.json In addition to IAM policies, NaviSite also employs encryption to protect data at rest and in transit. By encrypting data using strong encryption algorithms, organizations can prevent unauthorized access to sensitive data even if it is intercepted or stolen. NaviSite supports encryption of data stored in its cloud storage services, such as Amazon S3, Azure Blob Storage, and Google Cloud Storage. To enable encryption for an Amazon S3 bucket, organizations can use the AWS Management Console or the AWS CLI. Using the AWS CLI, organizations can use the "aws s3api put-bucket-encryption" command to enable default encryption for a bucket. For example, the following command enables AES256 encryption for a bucket named "example-bucket": aws s3api put-bucket-encryption --bucket example-bucket --server-side-encryption-conflguration

'{"Rules":[{"ApplyServerSideEncryptionByDefault":{ "SSEAlgorithm":"AES256"}}]}' Another important aspect of NaviSite's security framework is network security. NaviSite employs network segmentation and firewalls to control traffic flow and prevent unauthorized access to its cloud infrastructure. By *implementing network security groups and access control lists (ACLs), organizations can define rules that allow or deny traffic based on source IP address, destination IP address, port, and protocol. To configure network security groups in Azure, organizations can use the Azure portal or the Azure CLI. Using the Azure CLI, organizations can use the "az network nsg rule create" command to create a new network security group rule. For example, the following command creates a rule named "AllowSSH" that allows inbound SSH traffic on port 22: az network nsg rule create --name AllowSSH --nsg-name example-nsg --priority 100 --source-address-prefixes '*' --source-port-ranges '*' --destination-address-prefixes '*' --destination-port-ranges 22 --access Allow --protocol Tcp Additionally, NaviSite conducts regular security assessments and audits to identify and remediate security vulnerabilities and compliance issues. By performing penetration testing, vulnerability scanning, and compliance audits, NaviSite can proactively identify and address security risks before they are exploited by attackers. Furthermore, NaviSite provides security training and awareness programs to educate employees about security best practices and ensure that they are aware of their responsibilities for protecting sensitive data and resources. In* *summary, NaviSite's security framework and best practices encompass identity and access management, encryption, network security, security assessments, and employee training, enabling organizations to protect their data and resources from a wide range of security threats and vulnerabilities. By implementing NaviSite's security recommendations and following best practices, organizations can strengthen their security posture and mitigate the risks associated with cloud computing.*

Implementing identity and access management (IAM) in NaviSite is crucial for maintaining the security and integrity of its cloud infrastructure. IAM allows organizations to control who can access resources and what actions they can perform. One of the primary tools used for IAM in NaviSite is role-based access control (RBAC). RBAC enables organizations to define roles with specific permissions and assign those roles to users or groups. This ensures that users have the appropriate level of access based on their job responsibilities. In NaviSite, IAM roles can be created using the AWS Management Console or the AWS Command Line Interface (CLI). Using the CLI, organizations can use the "aws iam create-role" command to create a new IAM role. For example, the following command creates a new IAM role named "ExampleRole" with the specified trust policy: aws iam create-role --role-name ExampleRole --assume-role-policy-document file://trust-policy.json Once the IAM role is created, organizations can attach policies to the role to define the permissions granted to users or groups. IAM policies in NaviSite are JSON documents that specify the actions allowed or denied for a particular resource. Organizations can create custom IAM policies tailored to their specific security requirements or use managed policies provided by NaviSite or AWS. To attach a policy to an IAM role, organizations can use the "aws iam attach-role-policy" command. For example, the following command attaches the "AmazonS3FullAccess" managed policy to the "ExampleRole" IAM role: aws iam attach-role-policy --role-name ExampleRole --policy-arn arn:aws:iam::aws:policy/AmazonS3FullAccess In addition to RBAC, NaviSite also employs other IAM features such as multi-factor authentication (MFA) and identity federation. MFA adds an extra layer of security by requiring users to provide a second form of authentication, such as a one-time password generated by a hardware token or a mobile app, in addition to their username and password. Identity federation allows organizations to integrate their existing identity provider (IdP) with NaviSite's IAM system, enabling users to sign in using their existing credentials. This simplifies the user authentication process and allows organizations to enforce centralized access policies across their entire infrastructure. Another important aspect of IAM in NaviSite is the use of temporary security credentials. Temporary credentials are short-lived credentials that are dynamically generated and provided to users or applications when they need to access AWS resources. This helps reduce the risk of long-term credential exposure and unauthorized access. Organizations can use the AWS Security Token Service (STS) to generate temporary credentials for IAM roles. For example, the following command requests temporary credentials for the "ExampleRole" IAM role: aws sts assume-role -- role-arn

arn:aws:iam::123456789012:role/ExampleRole -- role-session-name ExampleSession Once the temporary credentials are obtained, users or applications can use them to access AWS resources until they expire. In summary, implementing IAM in NaviSite is essential for maintaining a secure and well-managed cloud environment. By leveraging features such as RBAC,

MFA, identity federation, and temporary security credentials, organizations can ensure that only authorized users have access to their resources and that sensitive data remains protected from unauthorized access.

Performance monitoring is a critical aspect of managing cloud infrastructure in NaviSite, ensuring optimal performance, identifying bottlenecks, and proactively addressing issues. NaviSite offers a variety of tools and techniques for performance monitoring, enabling organizations to gain insights into their system's health and performance metrics. One of the primary tools used for performance monitoring in NaviSite is Amazon CloudWatch. CloudWatch provides a comprehensive set of monitoring services for monitoring AWS resources and applications running on the AWS infrastructure. With CloudWatch, organizations can collect and track metrics, set alarms, and gain insights into resource utilization, latency, and error rates. CloudWatch Metrics are the foundation of performance monitoring in NaviSite, providing data points about the behavior of AWS resources over time. These metrics include CPU utilization, memory usage, disk I/O, network traffic, and more. Organizations can use CloudWatch Metrics to monitor the performance of their EC2 instances, RDS databases, Lambda functions, and other AWS services. CloudWatch Alarms are another essential feature for performance monitoring in NaviSite, allowing organizations to set thresholds on CloudWatch metrics and receive notifications when those thresholds are breached. This enables organizations to proactively respond to performance issues and prevent potential downtime or service disruptions. In addition to CloudWatch, NaviSite also offers enhanced monitoring capabilities through third-party tools and integrations. One such tool is Datadog, a cloud monitoring platform that provides real-time visibility into the performance of cloud infrastructure and applications. Datadog integrates seamlessly with NaviSite, allowing organizations to collect, visualize, and analyze performance metrics from a wide range of sources, including AWS services, custom applications, and third-party services. With Datadog, organizations can create custom dashboards, set alerts, and correlate performance data across different components of their infrastructure. Another popular performance monitoring tool used in NaviSite is New Relic, an application performance monitoring (APM) solution that helps organizations monitor the performance of their applications and services. New Relic provides deep insights into application *performance, including response times, throughput, error rates, and more. By integrating New Relic with NaviSite, organizations can gain visibility into the performance of their applications running on the AWS infrastructure and identify opportunities for optimization and improvement. Apart from these third-party tools, NaviSite also offers native monitoring and logging capabilities through services like AWS CloudTrail and AWS Config. CloudTrail provides a detailed record of API calls made to AWS resources, allowing organizations to audit and track changes to their infrastructure. AWS Config, on the other hand, provides a detailed inventory of AWS resources and configuration changes, enabling organizations to assess compliance, track resource changes, and troubleshoot issues. In summary, performance monitoring in NaviSite is essential for ensuring the reliability, scalability, and efficiency of cloud infrastructure. By leveraging tools like CloudWatch, Datadog, New Relic, and native AWS services, organizations can gain real-time insights into their system's performance, identify potential issues, and take proactive measures to optimize their infrastructure.*

Optimizing workloads for performance and efficiency is a crucial aspect of managing cloud infrastructure, ensuring that resources are used effectively and costs are minimized. One of the key strategies for optimizing workloads is right-sizing, which involves matching the resources provisioned to the actual requirements of the workload. In cloud environments like AWS, right-sizing can be achieved using services like Amazon EC2 instance types, which offer a wide range of instance sizes with different combinations of CPU, memory, storage, and networking capabilities. By selecting the appropriate instance type based on the workload's resource requirements, organizations can avoid over-provisioning and reduce costs. Another important aspect of workload optimization is implementing auto-scaling, which allows resources to be dynamically adjusted based on changing demand. In AWS, auto-scaling can be configured using services like Amazon EC2 Auto Scaling, which automatically adds or removes EC2 instances based on predefined scaling policies. By scaling resources up during periods of high demand and down during periods of low demand, organizations can ensure that they have enough capacity to handle workload spikes while minimizing costs during idle periods. Additionally, organizations can optimize workloads by leveraging AWS services like Amazon RDS for database workloads. Amazon RDS offers managed database services for popular database engines like MySQL, PostgreSQL, and SQL Server, providing features like automated backups, high availability, and scalability. By using Amazon RDS, organizations can offload the management of database infrastructure to AWS, allowing them to focus on developing applications and improving performance. Another important aspect of workload optimization is implementing caching strategies to reduce latency and improve performance. AWS offers services like Amazon ElastiCache, which provides fully managed caching solutions for popular caching engines like Redis and Memcached. By caching frequently accessed data in-memory, organizations can reduce the load on backend databases and improve application performance. Additionally, organizations can optimize workloads by using content delivery networks (CDNs) like Amazon CloudFront to cache and deliver content closer to end-users, reducing latency and improving the user experience. In addition to these strategies, organizations can optimize workloads by using AWS services like Amazon S3 for storage-intensive workloads, Amazon Aurora for high-performance database workloads, and AWS Lambda for serverless computing. By leveraging these services, organizations can offload infrastructure management to AWS and focus on developing *applications and delivering value to customers. Furthermore, organizations can optimize workloads by using AWS Cost Explorer to analyze usage patterns and identify opportunities for cost optimization. By understanding their usage patterns and optimizing resource allocation accordingly, organizations can reduce costs and improve efficiency. Overall, optimizing workloads for performance and efficiency is essential for maximizing the value of cloud infrastructure and ensuring that resources are used effectively. By implementing strategies like right-sizing, auto-scaling, caching, and leveraging managed services, organizations can improve performance, reduce costs, and deliver a better experience to end-users.*

*Leveraging automation tools for NaviSite Cloud
Services is essential for streamlining operations,
improving efficiency, and reducing manual errors.
One of the key automation tools used in cloud
environments is Infrastructure as Code (IaC),
which allows infrastructure to be provisioned and
managed through code rather than manual
processes. In NaviSite, infrastructure can be
provisioned using tools like Terraform, which
allows users to define infrastructure resources in
configuration files and then deploy them using the
Terraform CLI. For example, to provision a virtual
machine in NaviSite using Terraform, users can
create a Terraform configuration file defining the
VM's properties, such as its size, operating system,
and networking settings. Once the configuration
file is created, users can use the terraform apply
command to deploy the VM to the NaviSite
environment. By using Infrastructure as Code tools
like Terraform, organizations can automate the
provisioning of infrastructure resources, making it
easier to deploy and manage complex
environments. Another key automation tool used*

in cloud environments is Configuration Management, which allows the configuration of servers and applications to be automated and managed at scale. In NaviSite, configuration management can be achieved using tools like Ansible, which allows users to define the desired state of servers and applications in Ansible playbooks and then apply those configurations using the Ansible CLI. For example, to configure a web server in NaviSite using Ansible, users can create an Ansible playbook defining the desired configuration settings, such as the web server software to install, the configuration files to update, and the firewall rules to apply. Once the playbook is created, users can use the ansible-playbook command to apply the configuration to one or more servers in the NaviSite environment. By using Configuration Management tools like Ansible, organizations can automate the configuration of servers and applications, ensuring consistency and reducing the risk of manual errors. Another important automation tool used in cloud environments is Continuous Integration/Continuous Deployment (CI/CD), which allows code changes to be automatically tested, built, and deployed to production environments. In NaviSite, CI/CD pipelines can be implemented using tools like Jenkins, which allows users to define automated build and deployment workflows and then trigger them based on code changes. For example, to implement a CI/CD pipeline for a web application hosted in NaviSite, users can create a Jenkins pipeline defining the steps to build the application, run automated tests, and deploy the application to production. Once the pipeline is created, Jenkins can be configured to monitor the source code repository for changes and automatically trigger the pipeline whenever a new commit is made. By using CI/CD tools like Jenkins, organizations can automate the deployment of code changes, reducing the time and effort required to deliver new features and updates. Additionally, organizations can leverage monitoring and alerting tools like Prometheus and Grafana to automate the monitoring of their NaviSite environments and receive alerts when issues arise. By using automation tools for monitoring, organizations can proactively identify and address issues before they impact performance or availability. Overall, leveraging automation tools for NaviSite Cloud Services is essential for streamlining operations, improving efficiency, and reducing manual errors. By using tools like Terraform, Ansible, Jenkins, and monitoring tools, organizations can automate the provisioning, configuration, deployment, and monitoring of their NaviSite environments, enabling them to deliver value to customers more quickly and reliably.

Orchestrating workflows across NaviSite's Cloud Platform is a critical aspect of managing complex cloud environments efficiently and effectively. One of the key tools for orchestrating workflows in NaviSite is Kubernetes, an open-source container orchestration platform that automates the deployment, scaling, and management of containerized applications. Kubernetes allows users to define complex workflows using declarative configuration files called manifests, which specify the desired state of the application and its components. These manifests can include specifications for deploying containers, defining services, configuring networking, and managing storage resources. To deploy a Kubernetes application in NaviSite, users can create a manifest file describing the application's components, such as pods, services, and deployments, and then use the kubectl apply command to apply the manifest to the Kubernetes cluster. Once the manifest is applied, Kubernetes will automatically create and manage the necessary resources to ensure that the application runs as specified. Another tool for orchestrating workflows in NaviSite is Apache Airflow, an open-source platform for programmatically authoring, scheduling, and monitoring workflows. Airflow allows users to define workflows as directed acyclic graphs (DAGs), where each node represents a task in the workflow and edges represent dependencies between tasks. Tasks can be written in Python or other programming languages and can execute arbitrary code, making Airflow suitable for a wide range of use cases, including data processing, ETL (Extract, Transform, Load), and machine learning pipelines. To deploy an Airflow workflow in NaviSite, users can define a DAG file describing the workflow's tasks and dependencies and then use the Airflow CLI to deploy the DAG to the Airflow environment. Once deployed, Airflow will automatically schedule and execute the tasks according to the specified dependencies, providing visibility and control over the workflow's progress. Additionally, NaviSite provides integration with popular cloud-native tools like Terraform and Ansible, which can be used to orchestrate infrastructure provisioning and configuration management tasks. Terraform allows users to define infrastructure resources using code and then deploy them to the NaviSite environment using the terraform apply command. Ansible, on the other hand, allows users to define configuration management tasks as playbooks and then execute them using the Ansible CLI. By integrating these tools into NaviSite workflows, users can automate the provisioning and configuration of infrastructure resources, streamlining operations and reducing manual effort. Furthermore, NaviSite offers a range of managed services and APIs that can be used to orchestrate workflows across its cloud platform. These services include managed databases, serverless computing, and container orchestration platforms, which provide pre-built functionality for common use cases like data storage, processing, and analysis. By leveraging these managed services and APIs, users can quickly and easily integrate NaviSite's cloud platform into their existing workflows, enabling them to focus on building and delivering value to their customers. Overall, orchestrating workflows across NaviSite's Cloud Platform is essential for managing complex cloud environments efficiently and effectively. By leveraging tools like Kubernetes, Apache Airflow, Terraform, Ansible, and managed services, users can automate the deployment, scaling, and management of their applications and infrastructure, enabling them to deliver value to their customers more quickly and reliably.

Data governance and compliance are critical aspects of managing data effectively and securely in NaviSite Cloud environments. With the increasing importance of data privacy and security regulations such as GDPR, HIPAA, and CCPA, organizations must ensure that they have robust data governance and compliance practices in place to protect sensitive data and comply with legal and regulatory requirements. One key aspect of data governance is data classification, which involves categorizing data based on its sensitivity, criticality, and regulatory requirements. By classifying data appropriately, organizations can apply the necessary controls and security measures to protect it from unauthorized access, disclosure, or misuse. In NaviSite Cloud, organizations can use tools like AWS Macie or Azure Information Protection to automatically classify data based on its content and metadata, making it easier to enforce data governance policies and comply with regulatory requirements. Another important aspect of data governance is data access control, which involves controlling who can access, modify, or delete data within the NaviSite Cloud environment. This can be achieved using identity and access management (IAM) tools such as AWS IAM or Azure Active Directory, which allow organizations to define fine-grained access policies and roles to restrict access to sensitive data based on user roles, groups, or attributes. For example, organizations can use IAM policies to grant access to specific data resources only to authorized users or applications and deny access to unauthorized users or applications. Additionally, organizations can use encryption to protect data at rest and in transit within the NaviSite Cloud environment. This can be achieved using encryption services such as AWS Key Management Service (KMS) or Azure Key Vault, which allow organizations to encrypt data using encryption keys that they control and manage. By encrypting data, organizations can ensure that it remains confidential and secure, even if it is accessed or intercepted by unauthorized parties. Furthermore, organizations can use data loss prevention (DLP) tools to prevent sensitive data from being leaked or exposed outside of the NaviSite Cloud environment. DLP tools such as AWS GuardDuty or Azure Security Center can automatically detect and classify sensitive data, monitor data access and usage patterns, and enforce data protection policies to prevent data breaches or leaks. By implementing DLP controls, organizations can reduce the risk of data loss or exposure and maintain compliance with regulatory requirements. Additionally, organizations must have robust data retention and deletion policies in place to manage data lifecycle and comply with legal and regulatory requirements. This involves defining policies and procedures for retaining data for a specific period, archiving data that is no longer actively used, and securely deleting data that is no longer needed. In NaviSite Cloud, organizations can use services such as AWS Glacier or Azure Blob Storage lifecycle management to automate data retention and deletion processes, ensuring that data is retained and disposed of in accordance with legal and regulatory requirements. Furthermore, organizations should regularly monitor and audit their data governance and compliance practices to identify and remediate any potential risks or issues. This can be achieved using monitoring and logging tools such as AWS CloudTrail or Azure Monitor, which provide visibility into user activities, data access events, and security incidents within the NaviSite Cloud environment. By monitoring and auditing data governance and compliance practices, organizations can identify and address security vulnerabilities, policy violations, or unauthorized activities, helping to ensure the integrity, confidentiality, and availability of data within the NaviSite Cloud environment. Overall, data governance and compliance are essential aspects of managing data effectively and securely in NaviSite

Cloud environments. By implementing robust data governance practices, organizations can protect sensitive data, comply with legal and regulatory requirements, and maintain the trust and confidence of their customers and stakeholders.

Data backup, recovery, and archiving are critical components of any organization's data management strategy, ensuring data availability, integrity, and compliance. In today's digital age, where data is generated and consumed at an unprecedented rate, organizations must implement robust backup, recovery, and archiving solutions to protect against data loss, corruption, and unauthorized access. One of the key challenges in data management is ensuring the availability of data in the event of hardware failure, human error, or cyber-attacks. To address this challenge, organizations can use backup solutions to create copies of their data and store them in secure locations, ensuring that they can recover data quickly and efficiently in the event of a disaster. In cloud environments like AWS or Azure, organizations can use built-in backup services such as AWS Backup or Azure Backup to automate the backup process and protect their data against loss or corruption. For example, in AWS, organizations can use the AWS Backup service to create backup plans, schedule backups, and manage backup policies for their AWS resources using the AWS Management Console or the AWS CLI. Similarly, in Azure, organizations can use Azure Backup to back up virtual machines, databases, and file shares, and store backup data in Azure Blob Storage or Azure Backup Vault. By using these backup services, organizations can ensure that their data is protected and available when needed, minimizing the risk of data loss and downtime. In addition to backup, organizations must also have robust data recovery processes in place to restore data quickly and effectively in the event of a disaster. This involves implementing disaster recovery solutions that allow organizations to failover their applications and data to alternate locations in the event of a hardware failure, natural disaster, or other disruptive event. In cloud environments, organizations can use services such as AWS Disaster Recovery or Azure Site Recovery to replicate their workloads to secondary regions or data centers and failover seamlessly in the event of an outage. For example, in AWS, organizations can use AWS Disaster Recovery to create recovery plans, replicate their EC2 instances and EBS volumes to secondary regions using AWS Backup, and automate failover and failback processes using AWS CloudFormation or AWS CLI commands. Similarly, in Azure, organizations can use Azure Site Recovery to replicate their virtual machines, databases, and storage accounts to secondary regions or Azure Availability Zones and failover using Azure PowerShell or Azure CLI commands. By implementing disaster recovery solutions, organizations can minimize downtime and data loss, ensuring business continuity and resilience in the face of unexpected events. Apart from backup and recovery, organizations must also implement robust data archiving solutions to manage the lifecycle of their data and comply with legal and regulatory requirements. Data archiving involves moving data that is no longer actively used or accessed to long-term storage, freeing up valuable resources and reducing storage costs. In cloud environments, organizations can use services such as AWS Glacier or Azure Archive Storage to archive their data to low-cost storage tiers and retain it for long periods. For example, in AWS, organizations can use AWS Glacier to archive their data to cold storage, with retrieval times ranging from minutes to hours, depending on the storage class. Similarly, in Azure, organizations can use Azure Archive Storage to archive their data to the cool or archive tier, with retrieval times ranging from hours to days. By implementing data archiving solutions, organizations can reduce storage costs, optimize resource utilization, and ensure compliance with data retention policies and regulations. Overall, data backup, recovery, and archiving are critical aspects of any organization's data management *strategy, ensuring data availability, integrity, and compliance. In cloud environments like AWS or Azure, organizations can leverage built-in backup, recovery, and archiving services to protect their data against loss or corruption, minimize downtime, and ensure business continuity and resilience. By implementing robust data management practices, organizations can effectively manage their data lifecycle, optimize resource utilization, and mitigate the risks associated with data loss, corruption, and unauthorized access.*

Real-world examples of NaviSite cloud deployments provide valuable insights into how organizations leverage cloud technology to achieve their business objectives and address their unique challenges. These deployments span various industries and use cases, showcasing the versatility and effectiveness of NaviSite's cloud services in meeting diverse business needs. One such example is a large e-commerce retailer that migrated its online storefront and backend systems to NaviSite's cloud platform to improve scalability, reliability, and performance. Using NaviSite's cloud infrastructure, the retailer was able to handle spikes in traffic during peak shopping seasons, ensuring a seamless shopping experience for customers and maximizing sales opportunities. The retailer also leveraged NaviSite's managed services to offload routine IT tasks, allowing its internal teams to focus on strategic initiatives and innovation. Another example is a financial services firm that used NaviSite's cloud platform to modernize its legacy IT infrastructure and enhance data security and compliance. By migrating its applications and data to NaviSite's cloud, the firm improved agility and flexibility, enabling faster time-to-market for new products and services. NaviSite's robust security features, including encryption, access controls, and threat detection, helped the firm protect sensitive financial data and comply with industry regulations. Additionally, NaviSite's disaster recovery services ensured business continuity and resilience, mitigating the risk of data loss and downtime. In the healthcare industry, a large hospital system deployed its electronic health record (EHR) system on NaviSite's cloud platform to improve patient care and operational efficiency. By hosting its EHR system in the cloud, the hospital system gained access to scalable compute and storage resources, allowing it to store and analyze large volumes of patient data securely. NaviSite's compliance certifications, such as HIPAA and HITRUST, reassured the hospital system of its ability to safeguard patient information and comply with healthcare regulations. Moreover, NaviSite's disaster recovery solutions provided the hospital system with a robust backup and recovery strategy, ensuring continuous access to critical patient records and applications. In the manufacturing sector, a global automotive company leveraged NaviSite's cloud services to streamline its supply chain operations and improve collaboration with suppliers and partners. By migrating its supply chain management applications to NaviSite's cloud, the company achieved greater visibility and control over its inventory, production, and distribution processes. NaviSite's high-performance infrastructure and low-latency network connectivity enabled real-time data sharing and analysis, facilitating faster decision-making and responsiveness to market demands. Additionally, NaviSite's data analytics and machine learning capabilities helped the company identify trends and insights to optimize its supply chain performance further. These real-world examples demonstrate the transformative impact of NaviSite's cloud deployments on organizations across various industries. By leveraging NaviSite's cloud platform, organizations can drive innovation, improve operational efficiency, and achieve their business objectives more effectively in today's digital economy.

Insights from NaviSite cloud experts and thought leaders offer valuable perspectives on emerging trends, best practices, and innovative strategies for leveraging cloud technology to drive business success. These experts bring a wealth of knowledge and experience to the table, drawing *from their extensive backgrounds in cloud architecture, infrastructure management, cybersecurity, and more. By sharing their insights through various channels such as webinars, whitepapers, blog posts, and industry events, NaviSite's cloud experts help organizations stay informed and ahead of the curve in an ever-evolving digital landscape. One area where NaviSite's cloud experts provide valuable insights is in cloud migration strategies and planning. With their expertise in assessing application workloads, identifying dependencies, and mitigating risks, these experts help organizations develop comprehensive migration plans tailored to their unique needs and objectives. They offer guidance on selecting the right cloud deployment model, whether public, private, or hybrid, based on factors such as performance requirements, compliance considerations, and cost optimization. Additionally, NaviSite's cloud experts advise organizations on optimizing their cloud infrastructure for scalability, resilience, and security, ensuring a smooth transition to the cloud and maximum return on investment. Another area of expertise from NaviSite's cloud thought leaders is in cloud security and compliance. With the increasing prevalence of cyber threats and data breaches, organizations must prioritize security when migrating to the cloud. NaviSite's security experts provide insights into implementing robust security controls, such as encryption, access management, and threat detection, to protect sensitive data and mitigate security risks. They also offer guidance on achieving compliance with industry regulations, such as GDPR, HIPAA, and PCI DSS, through comprehensive security assessments, audit trails, and compliance reporting. By leveraging the expertise of NaviSite's cloud security specialists, organizations can build a strong security posture and maintain trust with their customers and partners. Additionally, NaviSite's cloud experts offer insights into optimizing cloud costs and performance. With the pay-as-you-go pricing model of cloud services, organizations must closely monitor their usage and spending to avoid cost overruns and inefficiencies. NaviSite's cloud cost optimization experts help organizations analyze their cloud usage patterns, identify areas for optimization, and implement cost-saving measures such as rightsizing instances, leveraging reserved instances, and implementing auto-scaling policies. They also provide guidance on optimizing performance through workload tuning, resource allocation, and network optimization, ensuring that organizations achieve the desired performance levels at the lowest possible cost. Overall, insights from NaviSite cloud experts and thought leaders empower organizations to make informed decisions, drive innovation, and achieve their business objectives in the cloud. By staying abreast of the latest trends, best practices, and industry developments, organizations can unlock the full potential of cloud technology and gain a competitive edge in today's digital economy.*

Conclusion

In summary, "Cloud Migration Mastery" offers a comprehensive and holistic approach to navigating the complex landscape of cloud integration. Through four meticulously crafted books, readers are equipped with the essential knowledge, advanced strategies, and expert tactics needed to achieve seamless cloud migration across leading platforms like AWS, Microsoft Azure, VMware, and NaviSite.

Book 1, "Cloud Migration Essentials: A Beginner's Guide to AWS," serves as a foundational resource for beginners, providing a clear roadmap for understanding the fundamentals of cloud migration and leveraging the powerful features of Amazon Web Services.

Book 2, "Mastering Microsoft Azure: Advanced Strategies for Cloud Migration," delves deeper into the advanced strategies and best practices for optimizing cloud migration on the Microsoft Azure platform. Readers gain insights into complex topics such as identity management, AI and machine learning services, and hybrid cloud solutions.

Book 3, "VMware Virtualization: Optimizing Cloud Migration for Enterprises," offers a comprehensive exploration of VMware virtualization technology and its role in optimizing cloud migration for enterprise environments. From vSphere architecture to performance monitoring, readers gain a deep understanding of VMware's tools and techniques.

Book 4, "Navigating NaviSite: Expert Tactics for Seamless Cloud Integration," rounds out the bundle with expert tactics and insights into cloud integration with NaviSite. Readers learn how to harness NaviSite's cloud services portfolio, navigate its industry solutions, and implement best practices for security, compliance, and performance optimization.

Together, these four books provide a complete guide to mastering cloud migration, empowering readers to overcome challenges, capitalize on opportunities, and unlock the full potential of cloud technology for their organizations. Whether you're a beginner looking to get started or an experienced professional seeking advanced strategies, "Cloud Migration Mastery" offers the knowledge and expertise you need to succeed in today's cloud-centric world.

www.ingramcontent.com/pod-product-compliance
Lightning Source LLC
Chambersburg PA
CBHW071233050326
40690CB00011B/2104